MODULE

magic

GINGER LUTERS

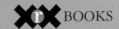

Module Magic PUBLISHED BY XRX BOOKS

PUBLISHER
Alexis Yiorgos Xenakis

MANAGING EDITOR
David Xenakis

EDITOR
Elaine Rowley

EDITORIAL ASSISTANT
Sue Nelson

EDITORIAL INTERN
Jasmin Karimzadeh

INSTRUCTION ASSISTANT
Cole Kelley

COPY EDITOR
Holly Brunner

GRAPHIC DESIGNER
Bob Natz

PHOTOGRAPHER
Alexis Xenakis

SECOND PHOTOGRAPHER
Mike Winkleman

PHOTO STYLIST
Rick Mondragon

PRODUCTION DIRECTOR &
COLOR SPECIALIST
Dennis Pearson

PRODUCTION
Everett Baker
Nancy Holzer
Susan Becker

TECHNICAL ILLUSTRATIONS
Jay Reeve
Carol Skallerud

SPECIAL DESIGN &
ILLUSTRATIONS
Natalie Sorenson

MIS
Jason Bittner

FIRST PUBLISHED IN USA IN 2004 BY XRX, INC.

ISBN 1-8937621-6-5

Produced in Sioux Falls, South Dakota, by XRX, Inc.,
PO Box 1525, Sioux Falls, SD 57101-1525 USA 605.338.2450

another publication of BOOKS

Visit us online at www.knittinguniverse.com

GINGER LUTERS

MODULE
magic

Creative
Projects
to knit

block at a time

GINGER LUTERS

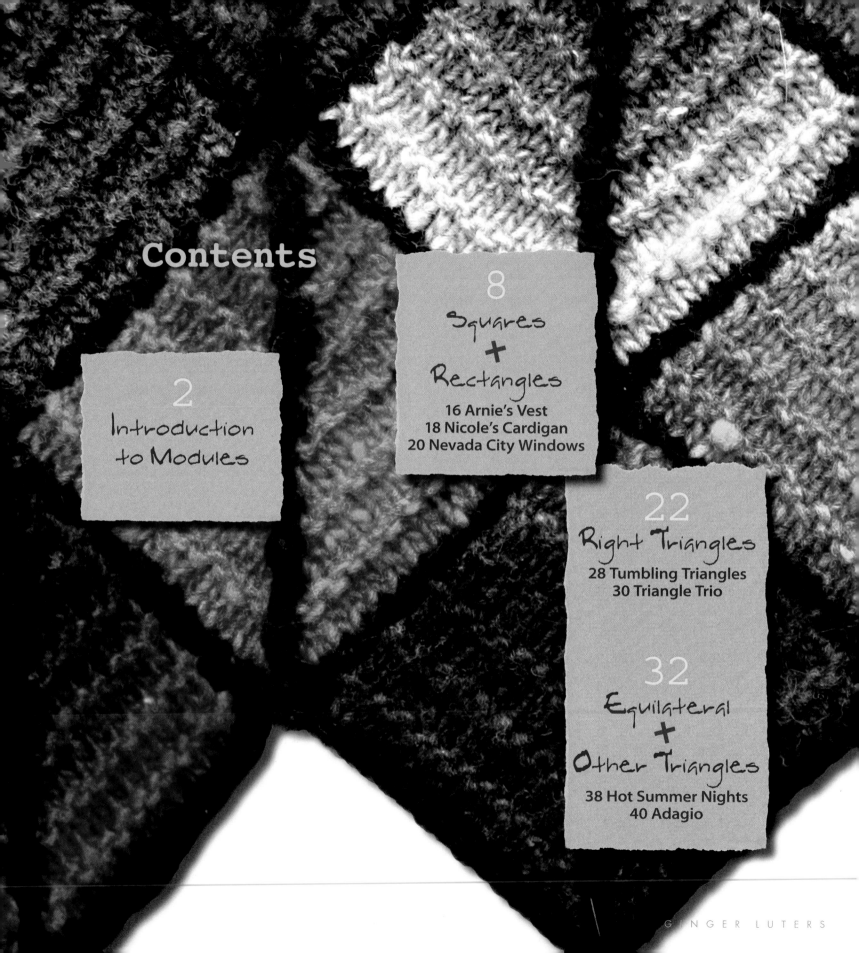

Contents

Grids

This book presents ideas for making fabrics and garments from modules. They can be knitted as presented, but you can also personalize them in any color, stitch, and texture you prefer. From there you can then design your own combinations.

The grids—blocks, diamonds, and triangles—lay a foundation that you can use to create a pattern you like. The garment silhouettes are shown alongside the grids to help you in your trek. Before you cast on a stitch, you can preview your design ideas on the grids. Arrange the blocks as you would arrange puzzle pieces, dominoes, blocks, or tiles. As you develop a design, you can add color or directional changes in the modules.

The arrangements have infinite possibilities, even squares can be arranged to form different modules. How you choose to combine them will be completely up to you.

The designs on paper can then be analyzed to see the sequence of knitting and the arrangement of modules. As you work many other ideas may occur to you.

The logic of modules is easy to comprehend, and the endless numbers of unique patterns are truly a treasure trove to explore.

Go ahead, see what you may conjure up—
It's truly magic!

introduction to modules

Module Magic—why is that the name of this book? The "module" part is obvious, but where does the "magic" come from? To me, the entire craft of knitting is magic. The fact that two sticks and some yarn can produce such diversity is endlessly fascinating and enchanting. One of the reasons I knit is because it offers so many directions in which one can learn, grow, and experiment. There is always something else to try, something new to learn.

My interest in modular shapes dates back to childhood when my favorite toy was a set of wooden blocks with solid colors on four sides. The other two sides had two colors, divided diagonally into two colored triangles. I would play with them for hours, arranging and rearranging, never realizing that years later I would do the same with knitted blocks.

I learned to knit at a young age and I always loved working with my hands and with fibers, but it wasn't until much later that my interest in geometry and modular units merged with my love of fibers. Brightly colored blocks and triangles began to appear in my small woven tapestries. Next I began to incorporate similar features into my knitting. Soon I was teaching knit design classes and publishing patterns for my colorful geometric sweaters. The more I worked with modular shapes, the more ideas I had for designs and techniques. I had discovered the magic of modules.

WHAT IS MODULAR KNITTING?

Modular knitting is the process of knitting several small shapes that are joined together to create a garment or other project. The small pieces can be knit individually and sewn together, but I prefer to join them as I go, picking up stitches on one edge of the piece I've just finished in order to begin the next unit. In this way, even very large projects usually require a minimum of sewing and finishing. In its simplest forms, modular knitting is suitable for new knitters, but complex designs can challenge experienced knitters.

Modular sections can be almost any shape: squares, rectangles, right triangles, equilateral triangles, long strips, mitered squares, diamond shapes, parallelograms. All of the shapes in a project might be the same, or several different shapes could be combined to create one larger design.

WHY KNIT MODULARLY?

Module knitting is fun and rewarding—it's a bit like solving a jigsaw puzzle, planning and knitting so the shapes fit together. I see progress quickly as the piece builds shape by shape. While I love knitting, I don't love having hundreds of stitches on my needles at one time. With modules, I usually work with no more than 25 or 30 stitches at a time. I'm always telling myself, "I'll just knit one more square (or triangle, or whatever shape) and then I'll start dinner."

Modular knitting is portable. I love to knit while I'm traveling, and I carry sections of modular knitting in my purse, pulling it out to work on whenever and wherever I have a few spare minutes.

My interest in geometric shapes goes back to early childhood

Sometimes, one module shape is all it takes—Yuba River, page 54

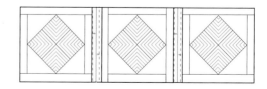

Other times several shapes are combined—Kalapaki Bay, page 94

Modular knitting loves color and so do I. It's an easy and excellent way to incorporate several colors and/or yarns into a single project. Handpainted yarns work especially well with modular knitting (page 74). The project might have many colors, but on any single unit, I knit with only one or two yarns at a time. Also, I often tell myself (feeling quite virtuous!) that I'm using up part of my yarn stash, but to be honest, as the project develops I often end up buying more yarn, more colors and textures.

Modular knitting is versatile The units can be combined in countless ways to create unique fabrics and garments. The overall effect can be subtle and sophisticated, bright and flamboyant, or quiet and conservative. It's up to you, the knitter, to choose the yarns, colors, and styles that suit your personal taste.

YARN CHOICES

My designs combine a variety of fibers. Practicality is usually the only limiting factor: no mohair in a summer sweater, but yes to cotton or rayon in a winter pullover. I try to keep the yarns for a project in one weight. They don't have to all be exactly the same weight, but within a narrow range: all Light weight, or all Medium weight (see page 120). You'll find that Light to Medium weight yarns with some loft, such as wools and mohair, work well in these projects. If I have some fine yarns that I want to combine with heavier yarns, I'll double the finer yarn or add a carrying thread. A swatch, or the first module, will show if it works.

YARN AMOUNTS

Because of the piece-by-piece and multicolored nature of modular knitting, it can be tricky to estimate the amount of each yarn required for a project. As always, there are several approaches to estimating yardage. Experience or finding a similar design and yarn, are good ways to start. You can use the similar design to approximate the total amount of yarn needed. If you are using more than one yarn, once you have this total yardage you will need to estimate the percentage of each yarn. Always be generous.

You can determine, for example, that 50% of your yarn should be purple, 30% olive green, and 20% rust. But modules can work to your advantage in several ways. It is easier and safer to add an extra color or a different dye lot than in most other kinds of knitting. And, since the modules may all be the same size or a related size (some modules twice as large as others, for example), you can determine precisely how much yardage or weight of each yarn is required to knit a module. Modular knitting is flexible enough to accommodate knitters who plan ahead and those who prefer to make choices as they go along.

NEEDLE CHOICES

The decision about which needles to use for a knitting project is a personal one. One knitter might prefer the warm texture of wooden needles, while another appreciates the speed and feel of metal needles. I use different needles for different projects, depending on the type of yarn I am using, as well as the stitch pattern. Some patterns require particularly sharp points, while some yarns might catch on wooden needles, or slip off of metal.

Star Light, Star Bright, page 92

T-Square, page 112

introduction to modules

Another choice is whether to work with straight or circular needles. I find that circular needles put less strain on my hands and arms, and I use them for nearly all my knitting. One exception is when I am knitting a lot of small modules, for example, a strip of small triangles. When I'm working with a small number of stitches, short straight needles are light and easy to handle. It all depends on what works best for you, which needles you enjoy working with, and which are most efficient for the particular project you have in mind.

Sizing the module

SIZE THE MODULE, SIZE THE GARMENT

How many times have you seen a sweater or jacket in a knitting magazine or book and thought that you would like to knit it, only to discover that the instructions didn't include your size? If you wear an XS or 1X, this scenario may be familiar. One bonus of modular knitting is the relative ease of charting a wider range of sizes.

A modular design can be sized by changing the size of the modules. This is the method I usually choose, and in most cases it is extremely simple. Modifying the stitch count of each module by 1 or 2 stitches can yield significant size differences. Stitches added or subtracted along one side of a unit add up as the module is repeated.

If you are knitting a sweater with 8 mitered squares across the front at a gauge of 4 stitches/inch, adding or subtracting 1 stitch along each side of the square will result in a difference of 8 stitches or 2" (4" for the sweater circumference).

This method of stitch-count alteration applies to most module shapes. In the case of mitered squares turned on their points, measure the increase or decrease in size diagonally across the square, from point to point. Right and equilateral triangles, squares that are knit straight (not mitered), rectangles, and strips all can be enlarged or reduced by adding or subtracting stitches on each side of the module.

Each of the 4 sizes of Yuba River, page 54, is achieved by adding or subtracting 1 or 2 stitches along each side of the mitered squares. To knit a smaller or larger size, simply add or subtract more stitches.

Mitered squares turned on their points

For large motifs that span the width of the fabric, decide how much wider or narrower you want your fabric to be (say, 1½" wider), then calculate the number of stitches this equals, based on your stitch gauge. If your gauge is 4 stitches/inch, you would make the piece 6 stitches wider.

A sizing method that doesn't involve the modules is to insert a panel on each side of the garment. The simple side panel, often knit sideways, can be as wide or as narrow as necessary to adjust the size. This technique can be especially useful in cases where the modular units are complex and changing stitch numbers becomes too complicated to be practical (Star Light, Star Bright, page 92).

For most designs with a small module, maintaining the unit's original size and simply adding or subtracting units on the sides (or center) of the garment is another option.

BLOCKING

Modular knitting benefits greatly from careful blocking. Combining different yarns, fibers, and stitches that are often oriented in various directions creates a knit surface that can be a bit unruly. It is important to evaluate your knitting as you go along and be certain that it is basically flat, needing only slight encouragement to lay perfectly flat. In most cases, blocking will not miraculously rescue a lumpy, bumpy piece of knitting. However, it will give work that has a few uneven areas a neat, professional finish.

I prefer to block the individual pieces of my sweaters before they are assembled. I begin by pinning them into shape (or I may use blocking wires). The next step depends on the yarns used, the amount of texture in the piece, and the amount of unevenness in the knitting. The lightest amount of blocking involves misting the surface of the knitting with water, then patting it firmly with my hand. More serious blocking can be done with a steam iron (or a Jiffy steamer) held about an inch above the piece, moving it over the entire area. For heavy blocking, I steam-press the piece, either with the iron or the steamer, using a pressing cloth if the yarn is at all delicate. Leave the knitting pinned into place until it is cool and dry.

KNITTING TECHNIQUES

For step-by-step directions for the techniques used throughout the book, see pages 116–119. However, there are five frequently used techniques that deserve special attention.

EDGE STITCHES

Many knitters tell me that they always slip the first or last stitch in a row, but I believe that it's better to evaluate the edge as well as the piece being knit, and then determine how to handle these edge stitches. This decision depends on what will happen to the edge later on and what stitch pattern is being used. The edge might be sewn to another piece of knitting, or stitches might be picked up in the edge stitches, or possibly the edge might not have anything done to it, as with the edge of some scarves.

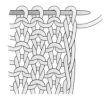

A slipped edge stitch makes it easy when picking up 1 stitch for every 2 rows

The fact to remember here is that when either the first or last stitch in a row is slipped, the resulting edge will have 1 stitch for every 2 rows of knitting in the main body of the piece. This works very well when you want to pick up 1 stitch for 2 rows of knitting, as when you are picking up stitches along the side edge of garter stitch or a garter ridge pattern. This does not work well if you have been working in stockinette stitch and want to pick up 3 stitches for every 4 rows of knitting. As a general rule, I slip the first stitch of every row if I am working in garter stitch or garter ridge stitch, using a solid color with no yarn changes. If I am changing colors (for example, 2 rows of yarn A and 2 rows of yarn B), I prefer to slip the stitches at the end of the row as follows: work until 1 stitch remains, bring the yarn forward and slip the last stitch purlwise. On the next row, knit into the back of the first stitch, then complete the row in pattern. Remember, if you need to pick up into more than every other stitch along the side edge of a piece of knitting, then work the edge stitches in stockinette stitch (or in your stitch pattern) rather than slipping these stitches.

introduction to modules

PICKING UP STITCHES

In this book, when you come to the words "pick up xx [number of] stitches," it means to "pick up and knit"; insert the right-hand needle into the right side of the knitting (unless the instructions say otherwise), wrap the yarn as for a knit stitch and pull this wrap through, forming a stitch on the right-hand needle. When picking up stitches along the side edge of a piece of knitting, I insert the needle 1 whole stitch in from the edge, rather than into the center of the first edge stitch. This gives a neater, cleaner line. When picking up along the top or bottom edge, I insert the needle just inside the cast-on or bound-off edge.

One other consideration here is the number of stitches to pick up along the side or top of a piece. As you know, knit stitches are not square, so a 1:1 pick-up ratio (1 stitch for 1 row) along the side of a piece of stockinette knitting would not be appropriate. In most cases the ratio for stockinette is 3:4 (3 stitches for 4 rows); that is, pick up 3 stitches and skip 1 row, along the entire edge. If the piece was worked in garter stitch, pick up 1 stitch for every 2 rows of knitting (1 stitch for every garter ridge). For other stitch patterns, you will have to experiment to determine the correct pick-up ratio. When picking up stitches along the top or bottom edge of the work, the ratio is 1:1 (1 stitch for 1 stitch).

DECREASES

Many of the techniques and projects in this book involve decreases: single decreases that slant to the right or left, or double decreases that eliminate 2 stitches in 1 operation. The simplest decrease is knit 2 together (k2tog). This single decrease slants to the right and is used when the edge of the fabric slants to the right, as in some right-angle triangles. When a purl version of this decrease is needed, simply purl 2 together (p2tog).

When the edge of the knit fabric slants to the left, use a left-slanting decrease. Among the several decrease options, I prefer ssk (slip, slip, knit 2 together): slip 1 stitch knitwise, slip the next stitch knitwise, then insert the left needle point through the front loops of the slipped stitches, and work a k2tog from this position. The purl version of this decrease, ssp, is worked by slipping 1 stitch knitwise, slipping the next stitch knitwise, sliding these 2 stitches back to the left needle and then purling these 2 stitches together through the back loops. I always tell my students that when they first work this decrease, if it doesn't feel awkward and strange, they're probably not doing it correctly.

When it comes to double decreases there are several choices. In most cases I prefer the decrease that leaves a single slipped stitch on the right side of the fabric. The knit version of this decrease is easy: slip 2 stitches together knitwise, knit 1 stitch and pass the slipped stitches over the knit stitch (S2KP2).

The purl version, S2PP2, is a bit more complex. Work it as follows: slip 1 stitch knitwise, slip the next stitch knitwise, slide these 2 stitches back to the left needle, then slip them both together purlwise through the back loops. Purl the next stitch and pass the 2 slipped stitches over.

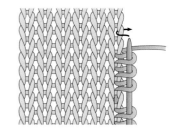

Picking up 3 stitches for every 4 rows

K2TOG

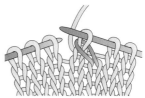

SSK

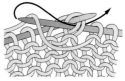

SSP

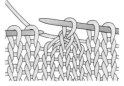

S2KP2

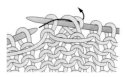

S2PP2

For more details see page 116

3-needle bind-off

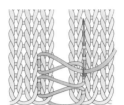

Mattress stitch

Left to right: Mattress Stitch; 3-needle bind-off in contrasting yarn, ridge to RS; Mattress Stitch on WS

Joining your knitting to stitches picked up along the edge of another piece. Left, p2tog at the end of a RS row; right k2tog at the end of a WS row

Joining by picking up stitches at the end of a knit row with p2tog decrease on the lower half and a k2tog decrease on the top half.

JOINING TECHNIQUES

There are times when it is necessary to join a module in-progress to one that is already knit. When this situation occurs, there are several options and no one right way. Each method has advantages and disadvantages; some are barely noticeable, others are quite decorative and emphasize the joining. Let's take a look.

One method is to finish the current piece and later join it to the other piece. If I want to make the join look exactly like the other edges, I sew it to the other edge with mattress stitch (or a variation thereof if I need to join the side edge to the cast-on or bound-off edge of another piece).

When I want to emphasize the line of the joined pieces, I use 3-needle bind-off and a contrasting yarn. Another option is to work mattress stitch on the wrong side, forcing the ridge that usually forms on the inside to the outside. This can be effective with finer yarns, but when heavier yarns are used, the ridge becomes quite bulky.

As I knit modules, I often join the finished section to the section I'm working on. With a spare needle I pick up stitches along the side edge of the finished piece using the yarn that will be used for the new piece. (If you know in advance that you're going to be using this method, use a chain selvedge stitch on the first piece of knitting for ease in picking up stitches every other row.) Then, as I work the new piece, on every other row I work the last stitch on my needle together with the bottom stitch on the holding needle. There are several ways to join these 2 stitches: knit 2 together, knit 2 together through the back loops, purl 2 together, or slip the last stitch knitwise, then knit 1 (the stitch that was picked up) and pass the slipped stitch over. Each method results in a slightly different look and I often try out several to see which works best for the situation. In most cases the slip, knit, pass slipped stitch over is neatest and least obvious. The bottom half of each joined area shows the result of slipping the first stitch on the row after the join is made. On the top half of the swatch, the first stitch was not slipped.

Finally, the piece in progress can be joined to another piece by simply picking up a stitch in the edge of the other piece. I use this pick-up-in-the-fabric technique least often, usually when a very small area needs to be joined or where it is difficult or impractical to pick up stitches. Note that the picked-up stitch adds a new stitch to the row, and therefore, some type of decrease is required or the piece will grow wider. One preferred decrease method in this situation is to knit to the last stitch on the needle, yarn forward, slip the last stitch, pick up a stitch purlwise in the edge of the other piece (insert the needle into the fabric from back to front), then pass the slipped stitch over. If the joined edge looks a bit loose, try slipping the first stitch on the next row.

Now, let's have some fun with modules!

squares + rectangles

squares ✚ rectangles

In the introduction, I mentioned my early fascination with simple geometric shapes and how I spent hours arranging colored blocks into various quilt-like designs. This early interest in geometric patterning carried over to my first explorations into knitwear design.

An important concept, an idea that has been fundamental to much of my work, occurred to me at this time. I began to view the outline or perimeter of a sweater as the outline of a canvas that could be filled in a variety of ways. I started with the idea of a basic square or rectangle for the front of a sweater and, as my skills grew, I modified these basic shapes to create more complex combinations.

At first I added simple squares of color, usually using an intarsia technique. Then, after looking at numerous quilting books and working on a few friendship quilts, I began to think about applying quilt-block construction to my knit designs, knitting each block rather than cutting fabric pieces as a quilter would. I continued to develop this technique of working with squares and rectangles, creating several variations and many sweater designs.

THE BASIC IDEA: BUILDING WITH BLOCKS

In its simplest form, this technique consists of knitting a randomly sized rectangle, binding off, rotating the rectangle 90°, picking up stitches, and knitting another rectangle with another yarn. For example, cast on enough stitches for a piece 3" wide, knit until it is 2" long, then bind off this 3" × 2" rectangle. Now, turn the rectangle sideways and, using another yarn, pick up stitches along its side. Knit for a while with the second yarn, then bind off. Rotate the piece another 90° so that the original rectangle is upside down, and with a third yarn, pick up stitches along the side of the second piece and the bottom edge of the first. You can see that it is possible to continue this process indefinitely, knitting larger and larger sections, each one attached to the previous sections. If you are familiar with quilt patterns, you can see that this technique lends itself to knitting the Log Cabin, as shown on page 13.

VARIATIONS ON BASIC SQUARES AND RECTANGLES

Once you understand the basic concept, there are all sorts of refinements and variations that can be introduced. You can create very simple or extremely complex patterns with this technique by varying color, yarn texture, and stitch pattern. Color changes can be used to achieve very different effects.

- Try combining blocks of a hand-dyed or variegated yarn with solid-color blocks, or shade from dark to light tones of a single color in each block.
- Use a group of monochromatic yarns with varying textures (such as all off-white in a shiny ribbon, a bumpy boucle, a smooth cotton, and a shaggy eyelash) or introduce stripes into some or all of the rectangles.
- Bright primary rectangles can produce a charming child's sweater, while subtly colored, monochromatic motifs might create a sophisticated adult's garment.

Knitting these squares and rectangles can be a perfect way to use up leftover bits of yarn. I often have this goal in mind, only to find myself buying more yarn to add to the mixture! If you choose one main yarn to intersperse throughout your project, or

Building with blocks

*Try stripes and ridges;
4 squares make 1*

Add slip stitches

Reverse the colors

Add interest with handpaints

Using a full-size paper pattern

to use as an outline yarn (see Tips, page 13) and for the bands, your yarn combination will appear more carefully planned and less like you were using up leftovers.

Another approach might be to introduce stitch patterns such as seed stitch, garter stitch ridges, or slip stitches. One important factor in choosing and combining stitch patterns is the variation in stitch gauge. You probably don't want your rectangles to pull in at the sides like an hourglass or to bulge out. There are ways to minimize the differences in stitch gauge. For example, if you want to insert a band of Fair Isle patterning in a stockinette-stitch rectangle, the Fair Isle section is likely to have a tighter gauge and pull in at the sides. To compensate for this change in gauge, add a few stitches to the Fair Isle section, or use a slightly larger needle, or both.

DESIGN APPROACHES

As with nearly all of the design approaches in this book, you can carefully plan a project, using graph paper or your computer, or you can gather a group of yarns and just start knitting. Part of this decision depends on your personality, your knitting skills and experience, and what makes you feel most comfortable. I use both approaches, depending on my mood and the initial idea for the project.

When I want to plan a project in detail, I often draw a full-size paper pattern (or print one using my computer and Garment Designer software), carefully arranging the placement of the colored blocks on each garment piece. Another option is to draw a precise outline of the garment on graph paper and plan the detailed design there. The grid sheets on pages 114 and 115 are a perfect design tool if you prefer the paper method.

If you are planning in detail the sizes and placement of squares or rectangles, remember that 1 stitch is lost on each edge of each piece in the process of picking up stitches or seaming. Also, the cast-on and bind-off rows are lost (and not counted in the measurement) in the same manner. These lost stitches can add up to several inches across the front of an entire sweater, depending on the size and number of blocks. Therefore, it is important to measure the size of each block 1 stitch in from each edge.

PICKING UP STITCHES

When picking up stitches along the edges of knit blocks, it is important to note the orientation of the stitches (the top, bottom, or side edges). On the top or bottom, stitches are picked up in a 1:1 ratio; that is, if there are 20 stitches across a bound-off (top) or cast-on (bottom) edge, pick up 20 stitches along this edge.

Along side edges, the pick-up ratio is different because knit stitches are not perfectly square (they are wider than they are tall). If you pick up stitches in a 1:1 ratio on side edges, too many stitches will be picked up and the new section will ruffle. In stockinette stitch, with most yarns and average stitch gauges, a pick-up ratio of 3 stitches for every 4 rows of knitting is usually correct. Trial and error may be involved; begin with the 3:4 ratio and check your work as you go along.

squares ✛ rectangles

Garter stitch compresses the row gauge, so pick up 1 stitch for every 2 rows of garter stitch (1 stitch for every ridge). In other stitch patterns, you may need to experiment to determine the correct ratio. One easy way to compute the correct pick-up ratio for any stitch pattern is to measure a swatch knit in that stitch pattern to determine both the stitch gauge and the row gauge. Then plug the gauge numbers into this sentence:
For every___(row gauge) rows of knitting, pick up ___(stitch gauge) stitches.
For example, if your gauge swatch has 5 stitches per inch and 8 rows per inch, then along the side of this piece pick up 5 stitches for every 8 rows, spaced evenly: * pick up 2 stitches, skip 1 stitch, pick up 2 stitches, skip 1 stitch, pick up 1 stitch, skip 1 stitch; repeat from *.

Picking up stitches along the side of a block

KEEPING IT SQUARE
Working with squares rather than random-sized rectangles can be another interesting exploration. Since knit stitches are not neat little squares (designing knits would be much simpler if they were), the shape of the knit stitch (wider than tall) must be considered when planning a knitted square. For a square 15 stitches wide, how many rows do you need to knit?

Obviously, you can simply measure, knitting until the piece is as tall as it is wide. But your gauge swatch provides the answer. Let's say the 15-stitch swatch is in stockinette stitch and measures 5" wide. Divide 15 by 3 and multiply the result by 4: 15 ÷ 3 = 5; 5 × 4 = 20; 20 rows will create a square.

4 rows

3 stitches

In stockinette stitch, the stitch-to-row (width-to-height) ratio is 3 to 4

When working in garter stitch, the math is even simpler because garter stitch compresses the knitting vertically, so that the width-to-height ratio is 2 to 1. Therefore, knit 2 rows for every 1 stitch cast on. This is easy to keep track of: just count the garter ridges and keep on knitting until you have as many ridges as cast-on stitches. With other stitch patterns, knit the first square until the height is the same as the width. Then check the stitch and row gauges to determine the correct ratio of stitches to rows for the pick-up.

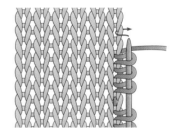

Picking up 3 stitches for every 4 rows

SMOOTHING EDGES AND JOININGS
While most squares and rectangles are joined by picking up stitches, you may occasionally come to a place where there is a slit between two sections that needs to be joined. You have two choices here: you can sew them together after the knitting is finished, or you can join the side edges of one strip to the next as it is knit.

There may also be small areas that need to be filled. Fill in these areas by picking up stitches on one edge or the other and knitting until the filler piece is even with the top edge. Or you could pick up on both edges and fill in this area with a mitered square (see page 44).

Filling in

SQUARES TURNED DIAGONALLY
Squares can be turned 45° to make diamond shapes. The edges can be filled in with triangles to square off the corners. To do this, knit a large square composed of small squares. Pick up stitches along one entire edge of the large square and knit back and forth, decreasing at the beginning and end of the row in 3 of every 4 rows

Turn a square of squares 45° and add triangles

in stockinette stitch or every other row in garter stitch. Repeat on each edge of the large square.

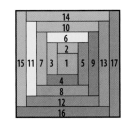

Knit the Log Cabin quilt block

LOG CABIN QUILT BLOCK

Begin by gathering two groups of yarns, one with light values and the other with dark values. Knit one small center square. Then pick up stitches along one side of this square and knit a rectangle half as high as it is long. The number of rows in this rectangle will be the same for the rest of the rectangles. Continue working around the center square, picking up stitches and knitting rectangles, placing the light and dark yarns as shown.

This motif could form an entire sweater front, or several small motifs could be sewn together, in the same way a quilt is constructed. The placement of the blocks can create interesting patterns (see a few on page 15). The blocks do not have to form an entire sweater; you might plan a sweater that is primarily solid-colored, with one quilt block for a pocket and another on the shoulder or sleeve.

TIPS

1. Evaluate your work as you go along. This applies to all of your knitting, not just to knitting squares and rectangles. Are the squares pulling in or ruffling up as you knit? After you finish each section, it's a good idea to lay it on a flat surface, pat it gently, and make certain that it will remain flat, that you like the color and shape, and that things are developing as they should.
2. Knit at a fairly firm gauge to help squares and rectangles retain their shape.
3. Block your knitting. You will find that blocking is especially important when working with modules because knitting in different directions and combining several yarns may result in unevenness that blocking will help resolve. See page 5 for a brief discussion of blocking techniques.
4. Outline each block with a contrasting color to achieve a stained-glass effect. Use the outline color to pick up stitches and to knit the next (wrong-side) row, creating a garter ridge. Then change to your main color and work the rest of the block. A strongly contrasting color such as black emphasizes the other colors used in each block.

Knit a stained-glass block

THE PATTERNS

As you've seen, combinations of squares and rectangles can be simple or complex, and are only limited by your imagination. The choice is up to you and the possibilities are seemingly endless. To get you started, here are three patterns based on rectangles and squares: Arnie's Vest, page 16 and Nicole's Cardigan, page 18, in a striped garter-stitch pattern, and Nevada City Windows, page 20, in a slip-stitch pattern.

squares + rectangles

WORK IT OUT
Use the square grid on page 114 to plan your own arrangements of blocks and colors.

Arnie's Vest, p. 16

Nicole's Cardigan, p. 18

Knit a square. Pick up stitches along one of its sides for another square. Repeat to create a 4-square block.

SWATCH TRICKS

Handpaint yarns and stripes of color or texture emphasize the change of direction from block to block. Slip-stitch patterns make the fabric look even more complex.

Knit Log Cabin quilt blocks and try different arrangements.

Arnie's Vest

Easy +

B [A]
LOOSE FIT

M (L, 1X)

Measures approximately
A 45½ (49, 52½)"
B 24¼ (26, 27¾)"

10cm/4"

20 ridges GET GAUGE!
        19

over garter stitch
(knit all rows)

1 2 3 **4** 5 6

Medium weight
A 350 (400, 450) yds
B 350 (400, 450) yds
C 240 (280, 310) yds

4mm/US 6
or size to obtain gauge

&

Stitch markers

NOTES

1 See *Techniques*, page 116, for ssk, S2KP2. **2** In these instructions, "pick up" means "pick up and knit". Pick up all stitches with RS facing. **3** Refer to Map for placement of Basic Squares, direction of work, and edges to be sewn. Shading on Map indicates a modified Basic Square; see additional instructions. **4** Vest can be made shorter by omitting the bottom row of squares or shortening the bottom band.

BASIC SQUARE

Row 1 (RS) With A, cast on (or pick up, depending on where you are on the Map) 16 (17, 18) sts.
Row 2 Knit.
Row 3 With B, slip 1 as if to purl (sl 1), knit to end of row.
Rows 4–32 (4–34, 4–36) Sl 1, knit to end of row, changing colors as follows: 1 row B, 2 rows A, 4 (4, 6) rows C, 2 rows A, 8 (10, 8) rows B, 2 rows A, 4 (4, 6) rows C, 2 rows A, 2 rows B, 2 rows A. With A, bind off. Basic Square measures 3¼ (3½, 3¾)" when joined to other squares.

BACK

Beginning with Square 1 and following the numbers on the Map, work Basic Squares (unshaded blocks) and work shaded squares as follows:

Square 22
Work 18 (20, 22) rows of Basic Square. Bind off.

Square 25
Work 18 (20, 22) rows of Basic Square. Complete Basic Square, AT SAME TIME, work ssk at beginning of every RS row.

Square 39
Work 18 (20, 22) rows of Basic Square. Complete Basic Square, AT SAME TIME, knit 2 sts together (k2tog) at beginning of every WS row.

FRONT

Begin with Square 1 and follow the Map, working shaded squares as follows:

Square 18
Pick up 8 (8, 9) sts in first 8 (8, 9) ridges of Square 17 Complete Basic Square, AT SAME TIME, decrease 1 st at beginning of every other WS row.

Square 20
Work in Basic Square pattern, AT SAME TIME,

decrease 1 st at beginning of every other WS row until 8 (9, 9) sts remain. Bind off.

Square 23
Work 16 (18, 18) rows of Basic Square. Bind off.

Square 34
Work as Square 20 EXCEPT decrease at beginning of every other RS row.

Square 37
Work 16 (18, 18) rows of Basic Square. Bind off.

Square 38
Pick up 8 (8, 9) sts in last 8 (8, 9) ridges of Square 17. Complete Basic Square, AT SAME TIME, decrease 1 st at beginning of every other RS row.

FINISHING

Sew right shoulder seam.

Neckband
Row 1 With A, pick up 43 (46, 49) sts from top of Front left shoulder to lower point of V-neck, pick up 1 st on top edge of Square 17 (place marker on this st), pick up 43 (46, 49) sts along right edge of V-neck to right shoulder seam, and 29 (31, 33) sts across Back neck—116 (124, 132) sts.
Row 2 Knit.
Row 3 With B, k1, * sl 1 with yarn in back (wyib), k1; repeat from * to 1 st before marker, S2KP2 (move marker to new center st), * Sl 1 wyib, k1; repeat from * to end.
Row 4 K1, * sl 1 with yarn in front (wyif), k1; repeat from *, end k1.
Row 5 With A, knit to 1 st before marker, S2KP2 (move marker to new center st), knit to end of row.
Row 6 Knit to center st, p1, knit to end of row.
Rows 7–9 Repeat Rows 3–5.
Row 10 Bind off.
Sew left shoulder seam.

Armhole edging
With A, pick up 115 (121, 127) sts around armhole. Work as for neckband, working S2KP2 in each underarm corner.

Bottom band
Row 1 With A, pick up 112 (119, 126) sts across bottom edge of vest Back.
Row 2 Knit.
Row 3 With B, k1, * sl 1 wyib, k1; repeat from *, end k1.
Row 4 K1, * sl 1 wyif, k1; repeat from *, end k1.

Simple squares, knit one at a time in garter stitch, are joined as you work,
resulting in a striking vest that grows quickly and is fun to knit.

Rows 5, 6 With A, knit.
Row 7 With B, k1, * sl 1 wyib, k3; repeat from *,
end sl 1, k1.
Row 8 K1, * sl 1 wyif, k3; repeat from *, end sl 1, k1.
Rows 9, 10 With A, knit.
Rows 11–14 Repeat Rows 3–6.
Bind off. Repeat for Vest Front.
Sew side seams, sew in ends. Block lightly.

——— Cast on
- - - - Pick up and knit
wwww Seam
——→ Direction of knitting
——— 3-needle bind-off

Back Map

	M	L	1X
Module Size			
Inches	3¼	3½	3¾
Stitches	16	17	18

Front Map

Basic Squares for a Large vest (right) and
1X vest (left): the extra rows change the
proportions of the stripes slightly.

BAABAJOES Wool Pak 8 Ply 1 skein each in color Charcoal (A), Natural (B),
and Tussock (C); shown i n Medium

Nicole's Cardigan

Easy +

LOOSE FIT

Child's 4 (6, 8)

*When buttoned,
measures approximately*
A 28½ (31, 33½)"
B 17½ (19, 20½)"
C 21 (22, 23)"

10cm/4"

21 ridges GET GAUGE!
20

*over garter stitch
(knit all rows),
using larger needles*

1 2 3 **4** 5 6

Medium weight
A 260 (290, 320) yds
B 260 (290, 320) yds
C 330 (370, 410) yds

*3.5 and 3.75mm/US 4 and 5
or sizes to obtain gauge*

Six 20mm/¾" buttons

NOTES

1 See *Techniques*, page 116, for cable cast-on.
2 In these instructions "pick up" means "pick up and knit." Pick up all stitches with RS facing and A. **3** Refer to Map for placement of Basic Squares, direction of work, and edges to be sewn. Shading on Map indicates a modified Basic Square; see additional instructions.

BASIC SQUARE

Row 1 (RS) With larger needles and A, cast on (or pick up, depending on where you are on the Map) 14 (15, 16) sts.
Row 2 Knit.
Row 3 With B, slip 1 as if to purl (sl 1), knit to end of row.
Rows 4–28 (4–30, 4–32) Sl 1, knit to end of row, changing colors as follows: 1 row B, 2 rows A, 4 rows C, 2 rows A, 4 (6, 8) rows B, 2 rows A, 4 rows C, 2 rows A, 2 rows B, 2 rows A.
With A, bind off. Basic Square measures approximately 2¾ (3, 3¼)" when joined to other squares.

BODY

Beginning with Square 1 and following the numbers on the Map, work Basic Squares (unshaded blocks) and work shaded blocks as follows:

Square 8
Work 18 rows of Basic Square. Bind off 8 (9, 10) sts at beginning of next (RS) row. Complete Basic Square on 6 sts.

Square 9
Pick up 9 sts and complete Basic Square.

Square 10
Work 16 rows of Basic Square. Decrease 1 st at end of next 3 RS rows. Complete Basic Square on 11 (12, 13) sts.

Square 11
Pick up 8 sts. Work 26 rows of Basic Square, AT SAME TIME, decrease 1 st at beginning of next 5 RS rows—3 sts. Bind off.

Square 12
Pick up 13 sts. Work 18 rows of Basic Square, AT SAME TIME, decrease 1 st on RS at beginning of every 8th row—11 sts. Bind off.

Square 16
Work 12 rows of Basic Square. Bind off.

Square 24
Work 19 rows of Basic Square. Bind off 8 (9, 10) sts at beginning of next (WS) row. Complete Basic Square on 6 sts.

Square 25
Pick up 9 sts and complete Basic Square.

Square 27
Work 13 rows of Basic Square. Bind off 9 (10, 11) sts at beginning of next (WS) row—5 sts. Work 2 rows even, then decrease 1 st at neck edge on the next 3 RS rows. Bind off.

Square 28
Pick up 13 sts. Work 18 rows of Basic Square, AT SAME TIME, decrease 1 st on WS at beginning of every 8th row—11 sts. Bind off.

Square 35
Work 11 rows of Basic Square. Bind off 6 sts at beginning of next (WS) row. Complete Square on 8 (9, 10) sts.

Square 38
Work 18 rows of Basic Square. Bind off.

Square 39
Pick up 9 sts and work 20 rows of Basic Square. Bind off 3 sts at beginning of next 3 WS rows.

Square 40
Pick up 13 sts. Work 7 rows of Basic Square, then bind off 1 st at beginning of next 3 WS rows. Complete Basic Square on 10 sts.

Square 44
Pick up 6 sts and complete Basic Square.

Square 51
Work 12 rows of Basic Square, then bind off 6 sts at beginning of next (RS) row. Complete Basic Square on 8 (9, 10) sts.

Square 53
Work 23 rows of Basic Square, then bind off 4 sts at beginning of next (WS) row. Bind off 1 st at beginning of next 2 WS rows. Complete Basic Square on 8 (9, 10) sts.

Square 54
Work 18 rows of Basic Square. Bind off.

Square 55
Pick up 9 sts. Work 20 rows of Basic Square, then bind off 3 sts at beginning of next 3 RS rows.

Square 56
Pick up 13 sts. Work 6 rows of Basic Square. Bind off 6 sts at beginning of next row, 3 sts at beginning

This simple pattern is an invitation to play with color. Notice how different it looks when compared to Arnie's Vest, page 16, on which it is based. While the basic design is the same, the squares are slightly smaller, there are fewer columns and rows, and the solid-colored sleeves enhance the squares.

of next RS row, then 2 sts at beginning of next 2 RS rows. Sew shoulder seams.

SLEEVES

Row 1 With A and larger needle, pick up 65 (67, 69) sts along armhole opening from underarm to underarm.
Row 2 Knit.

Change to C and stockinette st (knit on RS, purl on WS). Work 3 (3¼, 3¾)" even, then decrease 1 st at each edge of every 6th row 9 times—47 (49, 51) sts. Work even to approximately 15 (16, 17)".

Cuff

Row 1 Change to smaller needles and A, knit, decreasing 6 sts evenly spaced across row—41 (43, 45) sts.
Rows 2–4 Knit.
Row 5 With B, k1, * sl 1, k1; repeat from * to end.
Row 6 K1, * sl 1 wyif, k1; repeat from * to end.
Rows 7, 8 With A, knit.
Rows 9–12 Repeat Rows 5–8.
Bind off.

BANDS

Bottom Band

With A and smaller needle, pick up stitches and work as cuff, EXCEPT: Pick up 135 (145, 155) sts along bottom edge of body and omit decreases in first row.

Neck Band

Pick up 69 (71, 75) sts around neck edge and work as cuff, AT SAME TIME evenly space 4 decreases on Row 2 and 6 decreases on Row 11—59 (61, 65) sts.

Left Front Band

Note If sweater is for a boy, work Right Band first and make buttonholes in Left Front Band.
Pick up 77 (81, 85) sts along center Left Front and work as Cuff.

Right Front Band

Work as Left Front Band, inserting 6 buttonholes in Row 7 as follows: k4, yo, k2tog through back loops (buttonhole); [k12 (13, 14); work buttonhole] 3 times; work buttonhole; [k11 (12, 14); work buttonhole] 3 times; k2.

FINISHING

Sew sleeve seam, sewing straight part of sleeve to underarm edge. Sew on buttons to match buttonholes. Sew in ends and block lightly.

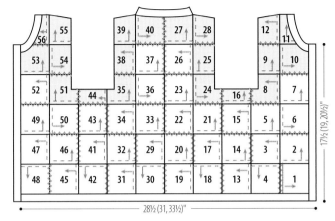

Body Map

Cast on
Pick up and knit
Seam
Direction of knitting

Module Size		
	4	6	8
Inches	2¾	3	3¼
Stitches	14	15	16

Sleeve

BAABAJOES Wool Pak 8 ply 1 skein each in colors Plum (A), Lavender (B), and Berry (C); shown in Childs' 6. See page 85 for another view.

Nevada City Windows

Intermediate

LOOSE FIT

S (M, L)

When buttoned,
measures approximately
A 37½ (43½, 49½)"
B 19½ (23¼, 26)"
C 28 (30, 32¼)"

10cm/4"

38
20
GET GAUGE!

over Basic Square pattern,
using larger needles

1 2 3 **4** 5 6

Medium weight
A 650 (790, 960) yds
B 590 (720, 870) yds

Five 25mm/1" buttons

4mm and 4.5mm/US 6 and 7
or sizes to obtain gauge

4mm/US 6
74cm (29") long

NOTES
1 See *Techniques*, page 116, for wrap and turn (W&T) for short rows. **2** Slip stitches as if to purl. **3** In these instructions, "pick up" means "pick up and knit." Pick up all stitches with RS facing and A. **4** Refer to Map for placement of Basic Squares, direction of work, and edges to be sewn. Shading on Map indicates a modified Basic Square; see additional instructions. **5** Sleeves are knit from side to side. **6** Back is worked in two pieces for ease of handling.

Garter Ridge Pattern
Rows 1, 2 With A, knit.
Row 3 (RS) With B, knit.
Row 4 With B, purl.
Repeat Rows 1–4 for Garter Ridge Pattern.

Band Pattern
MULTIPLE OF 2 STS PLUS 1
Row 1 (RS) With A and smaller needle, pick up required number of sts.
Row 2 Knit.
Row 3 With B, * k1, sl 1 with yarn in back (wyib); repeat from *, end k1.
Row 4 P1, * sl 1 with yarn in front (wyif), k1; repeat from *, end sl 1 wyif, p1.
Rows 5, 6 With A, knit.
Repeat Rows 3–6 for Band Pattern.

BASIC SQUARE
MULTIPLE OF 4 STS PLUS 3
Row 1 (RS) With A and larger needles, cast on (or pick up, depending on where you are on the Map) 23 (27, 31) sts.
Row 2 Knit.
Row 3 With B, k1, * sl 1 wyib, k3; repeat from *, end sl 1, k1.
Row 4 P1, * sl 1 wyif, p3; repeat from *, end sl 1, p1.
Rows 5, 6 With A, knit.
Repeat Rows 3–6 for a total of 42 (50, 58) rows. Bind off. Basic Square measures approximately 4½ (5¼, 6)" when joined to other squares.

RIGHT BACK
Begin with Square 1 and follow the Map, working shaded squares as follows:

Square 6
Work 9 (17, 25) rows of Basic Square. At the beginning of next WS row, bind off 18 sts. Complete Basic Square over 5 (9, 13) sts.

Square 7
Pick up 5 (9, 13) sts. Complete Basic Square.

Square 8
Work 16 rows of Basic Square. Bind off 6 sts at the beginning of the next row. Decrease 1 st at the beginning of each of the next 6 RS rows. Complete Basic Square on 11 (15, 19) sts.

LEFT BACK
Begin with Square 9 and follow the Map, working shaded squares as follows:

Square 13
Work 9 (17, 25) rows of Basic Square. At the beginning of the next row, bind off 18 sts. Complete Basic Square on 5 (9, 13) sts.

Square 15
Work 26 rows in pattern. Bind off 10 sts at the beginning of the next row. Decrease 1 st at the beginning of the next 6 RS rows. Complete Basic Square on 7 (11, 15) sts.

Square 16
Work 9 (17, 25) rows of Basic Square. Bind off. Sew center Back seam.

LEFT FRONT
Begin with Square 17 and follow the Map, working shaded squares as follows:

Square 21
Work 22 rows of Basic Square. Complete Basic Square, AT SAME TIME, decrease 1 st at the end of Row 23 and every 4th row—18 (20, 22) sts. Bind off.

Square 22
Work as Right Back, Square 6.

Square 23
Work as Right Back, Square 7.

Square 24
Work 18 rows of Basic Square. Bind off 6 (10, 14) sts at the beginning of the next row—17 sts. Bind off 3 sts at beginning of next 5 RS rows then 1 st at beginning of last RS row. Fasten off.

The squares in this jacket are joined as you work this fun-to-knit slip stitch pattern. The beautiful colors in the hand-dyed yarn appear to peek through little windows outlined in black. You can use the colors just as they come from the skein, or you can "cheat" and arrange them as you please. I did some color arranging and this takes a bit more yarn.

RIGHT FRONT

Begin with Square 25 and follow the Map, working shaded squares as follows:

Square 29
Work as Left Back, Square 13.

Square 30
Work 36 (40, 44) rows of Basic Square. At beginning of next 3 (5, 7) RS rows, bind off 4 (3, 3) sts. Complete Basic Square on 11 (12, 10) sts. Bind off.

Square 31
Pick up 19 sts. Work in Basic Square pattern, AT SAME TIME, decrease 1 st at the beginning of every RS row until 11 sts remain. Work even for 25 (34, 42) rows. Bind off.

Square 32
Work as Left Back, Square 16.

SLEEVES

Row 1 (RS) With A and larger needle, cast on 81 (84, 87) sts (counts as Row 1 of Garter Ridge Pattern).

Row 2 Knit.

Continue in Garter Ridge Pattern and work short-row shaping as follows:

Short Rows 3, 4 With B, k16, wrap next st and turn (W&T); purl to end.

Short Rows 5, 6 With A, k20, W&T; knit to end.

Short Rows 7, 8 With B, k24, W&T; purl to end.

Short Rows 9, 10 With A, k28, W&T; knit to end.

Short Rows 11, 12 With B, k32, W&T; purl to end.

Continue working 4 more sts every RS row until all sts have been worked.

Work 60 (72, 80) rows in Garter Ridge Pattern over all sts. Then reverse short row shaping, working 4 fewer sts every RS row until 16 sts remain on left needle. With A, knit 2 rows over all sts, then bind off.

Cuffs
Picking up 33 (41, 45) sts, work 22 rows in Band Pattern. Bind off.

FINISHING

Block each piece. Sew shoulder seams. Sew top of sleeves to armhole, sewing straight part of sleeve sides to underarm edge.
Sew sleeve and side seams.

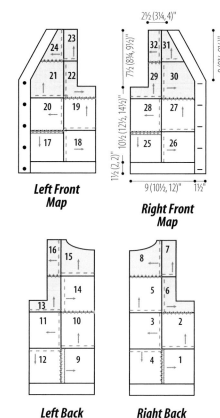

Left Front Map

Right Front Map

2½ (3¼, 4)"

7½ (8¾, 9½)"

8 (8¾, 9½)"

10½ (12½, 14½)"

1½ (2, 2)"

9 (10½, 12)"   1½"

Left Back Map

Right Back Map

——— Cast on
- - - - Pick up and knit
〰〰〰 Seam
⟶ Direction of knitting

6½ (8¼, 9)"

2"

20¼ (21, 21¾)"

Sleeve

15 (17½, 19)"

Module Size

	S	M	L
Inches	4½	5¼	6
Stitches	23	27	31

Bottom band
Picking up 184 (216, 248) sts across bottom edge of body, work Band Pattern for a total of 18 (22, 22) rows. Bind off loosely.

Front and neck band
Pick up as follows: 60 (72, 82) sts along Right center Front, place marker (pm), 32 (40, 48) sts from beginning of Front neck shaping up to shoulder seam, 37 (39, 41) sts across Back neck, 32 (40, 48) sts along right Front neck shaping, pm, and 60 (72, 82) sts down Left center Front—221 (263, 301) sts.

Work 18 rows in Band Pattern, working 2 increases at each center Front marker on rows 5 and 9, AT SAME TIME, on Row 9, work buttonholes as follows:

Row 9 K8, (9, 10), bind off 3, * k8 (10, 12), bind off 3; repeat from * 3 more times.

Next row Cast on 3 sts at each place that 3 sts were bound off for the buttonholes. Bind off. Sew on buttons to match buttonholes. Sew in ends and block lightly.

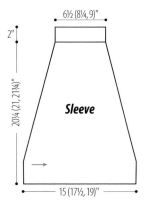

BROWN SHEEP Nature Spun 3 (4, 4) skeins in Pepper NS601 (A); NORO Kureyon 6 (7, 8) skeins in color 40 (B); shown in Medium

right triangles

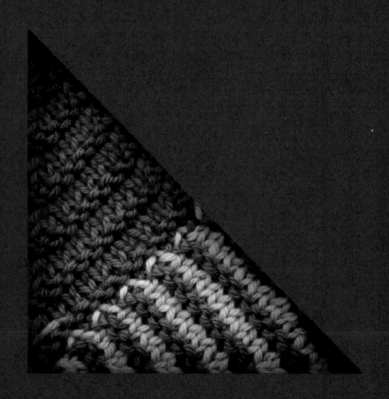

right triangles

Triangles have long been one of my favorite design shapes. They provide so many exciting possibilities, from right-angle triangles to equilateral triangles to various irregularly shaped units. My childhood blocks had colored triangles on four sides. Later, when I was in high school, I was very fond of geometry class…it was those triangles again!

KNITTING A RIGHT-ANGLE TRIANGLE
As I began designing with modules, I discovered that triangles were easy to knit, and nearly as easy to join into intriguing design units. Let's begin by taking a look at right-angle triangles. If the two short sides are the same length, these triangles have one 90° angle and two 45° angles. To begin, cast on stitches for one of the short sides.

• Calculate the number of stitches to cast on by multiplying the length of the short edge times your stitch gauge. For example, if your gauge is 5 stitches/inch and you want this triangle to be 4" along one short edge, cast on 20 stitches.
• After casting on (Row 1), I usually knit back across the wrong side (Row 2) to form a garter stitch ridge, which emphasizes the shape of the triangle.
• Continue to knit Triangle A (top) in garter stitch, working decreases on the left edge of the triangle on every other row (right-side rows). I prefer to place decreases 1 stitch in from the edge, which creates a smooth edge that is easier to work with later. Knit across the next row (right-side Row 3) to the last 3 stitches, k2tog, k1. Row 4 does not have any decreases.
• Continue working decreases on every other row until 2 stitches remain. K2tog, cut the yarn, and pull it through the last loop.

If you want the long edge (hypotenuse) of the triangle to face the other way, work the decreases on the right edge of the triangle (Triangle B). In Triangle A, the shaped edge slants from left to right, so k2tog decreases are used because they slant to the right. In Triangle B, the edge slants to the left, so a left-slanting decrease (I prefer ssk) is used.

BUILDING RIGHT TRIANGLES INTO SQUARES
Now, say you've knit a left-slanting triangle (Triangle 1) and you want to create another triangle that is joined onto it. Pick up stitches along the short side and knit another triangle. Since the short side is the same length as the cast-on edge, pick up the same number of stitches as were cast-on and knit a triangle just like Triangle 1— call it Triangle 2. Then pick up stitches along Triangle 2 and knit Triangle 3. Finally, pick up stitches on 3 and knit Triangle 4. Sew the short edge of 4 to the cast on edge of 1. You've knit a square composed of four smaller triangles.

This process can be the basis of many designs; see page 30 for a Trio of pillows. You can put stripes into each triangle, knit two triangles of one color and two of another, use a contrasting color yarn to cast on or pick up and knit the foundation rows, or join more triangles for larger motifs. Imagine the triangles on pillow tops, purses or tote bags, afghan panels, or panels for vest or jacket fronts and backs.

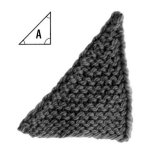

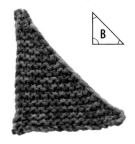

A right triangle can be decreased on the left edge…

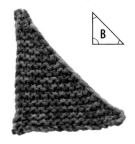

…or on the right edge

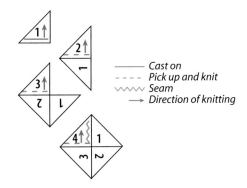

—————— Cast on
- - - - - Pick up and knit
∿∿∿∿ Seam
———→ Direction of knitting

Building triangles into squares

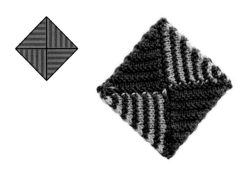

Add stripes

Alternate colors

Outline the triangles

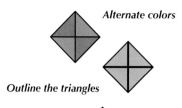

Join more triangles for a larger motif

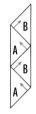

Building triangles into strips

A right triangle can also be cast on along the hypotenuse and decreased at both edges

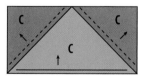

3 of these triangles form a Flying Geese motif

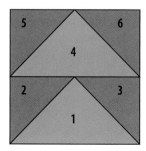

Repeating the motifs

BUILDING RIGHT TRIANGLES INTO STRIPS

Alternating one Triangle A with one Triangle B creates the strip of joined triangles that is the basis of the Tumbling Triangles Shawl, page 28. Stripes and color or texture changes offer a variety of effects.

Finally, what if you want to knit these triangles in a stitch pattern other than garter stitch? To knit Triangle A in stockinette stitch, work decreases on the left edge of the triangle on 3 of every 4 rows. After casting on and knitting one row, knit across the next row (right-side) to the last 3 stitches, k2tog, k1, and turn your work. Row 4 is a purl row and must include a decrease, so p1, p2tog, then purl across the row. Row 5 is another decrease row, so repeat Row 1. Row 6, a purl row, does not have any decreases. Continue working decreases on 3 of every 4 rows until 2 stitches remain. K2tog (or p2tog, depending on which side of the work you are on), cut the yarn, and pull it through the last loop. If you choose another stitch pattern, you'll need to find the decrease ratio that creates a right-angle triangle. Remember the stitch-to-row ratio, page 12.

BEGINNING WITH THE HYPOTENUSE

For more design possibilities, cast on an odd number of stitches along the hypotenuse (long edge) of the triangle and work decreases on both edges (Triangle C). The decrease ratio is the same: on 3 of every 4 rows for stockinette stitch. Be sure to work the appropriate decreases (right-slanting or left-slanting) on each edge of the piece. To form a neat point, work until 5 stitches remain and you're ready to begin a right-side row. K1, work a double decrease (I use S2KP2), then knit 1. On the next right-side row, work a double decrease, cut the yarn, and pull it through the last loop.

You can knit one Triangle C, pick up stitches along the short edges and knit smaller triangles. The result is a rectangle composed of triangles, the pattern called Flying Geese in the quilt world.

Motifs can be stacked (pick up stitches along the top of this rectangle, knit another large triangle followed by two more small triangles), for as long as you wish. The only tricky part is figuring out how many stitches to pick up along the short edge of Triangle C. The Pythagorean theorem is the basis of this computation, but you can simply divide the number of stitches along the bottom (long) edge of the triangle by 1.4. So, if the bottom edge of the triangle is 27 stitches wide, divide 27 by 1.4, which equals 19.28. Remember that an odd number will be needed for the next triangle, so drop the .28 and pick up 19 stitches along the short edge.

Or, if you know how many stitches are on the short side of a right-angle triangle (say, the stitches cast on for Triangle A), and you want to determine the number of stitches along the hypotenuse, multiply by 1.4.

THE PATTERNS

Two patterns are presented here to get you started. The Triangle Trio, page 30, is a simple pillow knit three ways. Tumbling Triangles, page 28, is a shawl pattern knit with a subtly colored hand-dyed yarn.

right △ triangles

WORK IT OUT

Use the grid on page 114 to plan shawls, pillows, and other designs.

Triangle Trio, p. 30

Tumbling Triangles, p. 28

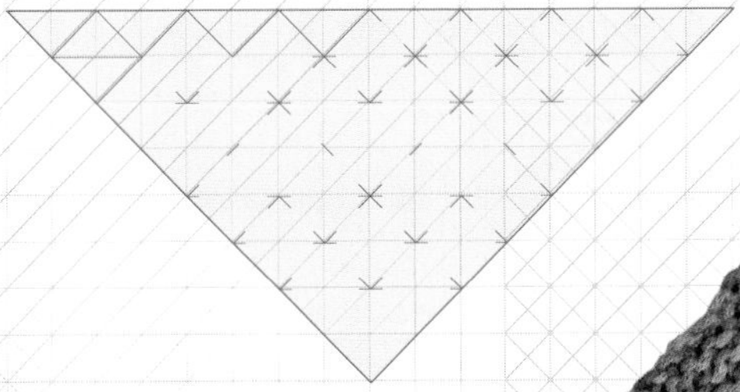

Pick up stitches along the straight side of a triangle and see what happens.

Imagine one color
only for a giant
rickrack scarf

SWATCH TRICKS
Work small triangles, or double
their size, or mix them together.

Knit a black triangle.
Add two white ones—
you just zigged.
Work 2 more in black—
you zagged.

Tumbling Triangles

Easy

One Size
Measures approximately
64" across top edge
30" from point to top

10cm/4"

13 ridges ▦ GET CLOSE
13

over garter stitch,
(knit all rows),
using 8mm/US 11 needle

🧵**1** 2 3 4 5 6

Super Fine weight, used double

A 660 yds
B 800 yds

OR

1 2 **3** 4 5 6

Light weight

A 375 yds
B 450 yds

6.5 and 9mm/US 10.5 and 13
74cm (29") long

8mm/US 11
or size to obtain gauge

NOTES

1 See *Techniques*, page 116, for ssk, sewn bind-off, and knit through back loop (tbl). *2* In these instructions, "pick up" means "pick up and knit." Pick up all stitches with RS facing. *3* Refer to Map for placement and color of Small and Large Triangles and direction of work. *4* Shawl is knit with a super-fine yarn held double throughout (this is one way to break up the color in a handpainted yarn). If using a heavier yarn, work a single strand.

SMALL B TRIANGLE

Row 1 (RS) With straight needle and B, cast on (or pick up, depending on where you are on the Map) 18 sts.
Row 2 Knit to 1 st remaining, slip 1 as if to purl and with yarn to RS (sl 1).
Row 3 K1 through back loop (tbl), knit to 3 sts remaining, k2tog, sl 1.
Row 4 K1 tbl, knit to 1 st remaining, sl 1.
Repeat Rows 3 and 4 to 2 sts remaining, k2tog. Fasten off. Small Triangle measures approximately 5½" wide when joined to other triangles.

SMALL A TRIANGLE

Row 1 (RS) With straight needle and A, pick up 18 sts.
Row 2 Knit to 1 st remaining, sl 1.
Row 3 (RS) K1 tbl, ssk, knit to 1 st remaining, sl 1.
Row 4 K1 tbl, knit to 1 st remaining, sl 1.
Repeat Rows 3 and 4 until 2 sts remain, k2tog. Fasten off.

LARGE TRIANGLES

Work as Small Triangles except cast on or pick up 36 sts instead of 18. Large Triangle measures approximately 11" wide when joined to other triangles.

LORNA'S LACES Helen's Lace 1 skein each in color Navy 24ns (A) and color Mixed Berries 38 (B)

Soft and drapey, this colorful shawl showcases the simple beauty of the triangle. Knitting begins at the top edge of the shawl, alternating strips of small and large right-angle triangles (if you prefer, you may use just one size of triangle). The shawl can be made as large as desired by adding more triangles and strips.

SHAWL

TIER 1 Beginning with Triangle 1 and following the numbers on the Map, work Small Triangles 1–15, alternating B Triangles and A Triangles.

TIER 2 Triangle 16 Work Small B Triangle, except join to the first A Triangle of the preceding strip as follows: At the end of each RS row, slip the last st, pick up 1 st in the edge of Triangle 2, and pass the slipped st over. On WS rows, sl 1 (as if to knit), then knit to 1 st remaining, sl 1.

Work Small Triangles 17–28, joining B Triangles to the A Triangles of the first strip at the end of every RS row.

TIER 3 Work Large Triangles 29–33, alternating B and A Triangles and joining B Triangles to A Triangles of the preceding strip.

TIERS 4, 5 Work Small Triangles 34–45, alternating B and A Triangles and joining B Triangles to A Triangles of the preceding strip.

TIER 6 Work Large Triangle 46, joining B Triangle to A Triangles of the preceding strip.

SHAWL EDGING

Row 1 With A and smaller circular needle, pick up 140 sts along edge X–Y, to just around the corner at Y with the last 3 sts picked up.

Row 2 Knit.

Short Rows 3, 4 K5, turn work (T); k5.

Short Rows 5, 6 K4, T, k4.

Short Rows 7, 8 K3, T, k3.

Short Rows 9, 10 K2, T, k2.

Short Rows 11, 12 K1, T, k1.

Short Rows 13, 14 Bind off 5 sts, k4—total of 5 sts on right needle, T, k5.

Repeat Short Rows 5–14 along edge X–Y.

Edge Y–Z Continue picking up 135 sts along edge Y–Z, working edging. After the last bind-off, pick up 1 st at Z, pass the last bound-off st over the picked-up st. Fasten off.

Edge Z–X With A, and smaller circular needle, pick up 144 sts along edge Z–X. Knit 1 row. Change to larger circular needle, knit 1 row, then work sewn bind-off.

FINISHING

Sew in ends and block, pinning each point of edging.

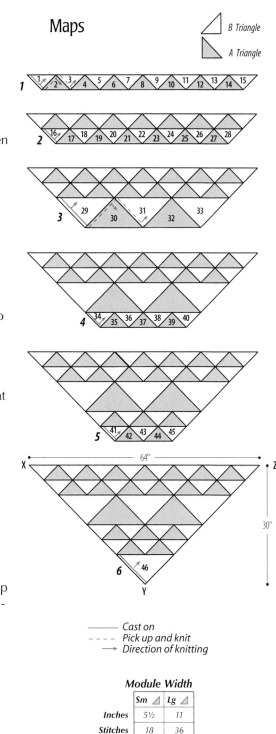

Maps

B Triangle

A Triangle

----------- Cast on
- - - - Pick up and knit
⟶ Direction of knitting

Module Width

	Sm △	Lg △
Inches	5½	11
Stitches	18	36

Triangle Trio

NOTES

1 See *Techniques*, page 116, for single crochet (sc), and backwards crochet. *2* In these instructions, "pick up" means "pick up and knit." Pick up all stitches with RS facing. *3* Refer to Map for placement of Triangles and direction of work. *4* See pillow back options, page 113. *5* Yarn allowance is for pillow front, additional yarn will be required to knit a pillow back.

Garter Ridge Pattern
Rows 1, 2 With A, knit.
Row 3 (RS) With B, knit.
Row 4 With B, purl.
Repeat Rows 1–4 for Garter Ridge Pattern.

SOLID-COLORED PILLOW
Triangle 1
Row 1 (RS) With CC, cast on 38 sts.
Row 2 Knit.
Rows 3, 5 Knit to last 3 sts, k2tog, k1.
Row 4 Purl.
Row 6 Knit.
Rows 7–10 Repeat Rows 3–6.
Change to MC and repeat Rows 3–6 until 2 sts remain, ending with a WS row.
Next row (RS) K2tog. Fasten off.
Triangles 2, 3, 4
Work as Triangle 1, beginning by picking up 38 sts as shown on Map.
Finishing
Sew Triangle 4 to cast-on edge of Triangle 1. With crochet hook and CC yarn, work 1 row single crochet (sc) and 1 row backwards crochet around outside edge of pillow. Sew in ends and block lightly. With sewing thread and needle, whipstitch knit pillow top onto cover of pillow form.

STRIPED PILLOW
Triangle 1
Row 1 (RS) With MC, cast on 38 sts.
Row 2 Knit.
Row 3 With CC, knit to last 3 sts, k2tog, k1.
Row 4 Purl.
Row 5 With MC, knit to last 3 sts, k2tog, k1.
Row 6 Knit.
Repeat Rows 3–6 until 2 sts remain, ending with a WS row.

Next row K2tog. Fasten off.
Triangles 2, 3, 4
Work as Triangle 1, beginning by picking up 38 sts as shown on Map.
Finishing
Work as Solid-colored Pillow, using MC yarn.

CHECKED PILLOW
Note Slip sts purlwise and with yarn to WS.
Triangle 1
Row 1 (RS) With MC, cast on 38 sts.
Row 2 Knit.
Row 3 With CC, k1, sl 1, * k3, sl 1; repeat from * to last 3 sts, k2tog, k1.
Row 4 Purl the purl sts and slip the slipped sts.
Rows 5, 6 With MC, knit.
Row 7 With CC, * k3, sl 1; repeat from * to last 3 sts, k2tog, k1.
Row 8 Repeat Row 4.
Row 9 With MC, knit.
Repeat Rows 2–9 until 2 sts remain, ending with a WS row.
Next row (RS) K2tog. Fasten off.
Triangles 2, 3, 4
Work as Triangle 1, beginning by picking up 38 sts as shown on Map.
Finishing
Work as Solid-colored Pillow, using MC yarn.

To knit a larger or smaller pillow top:
1. Determine your stitch gauge (for example, 4.25 sts/inch).
2. Determine the size of your pillow top (for example, 16" × 16").
3. Divide pillow top size in half (16" ÷ 2 = 8").
4. Multiply this by 1.4 (8" × 1.4 = 11.2"). This number is the length in inches from the center of the pillow to one corner.
5. Multiply this number by your stitch gauge (11.2" × 4.25 = 47.6). Round up to the nearest even number (in this case, 48 or for Checked Pillow, the nearest multiple of 4 + 2); this is the number of sts to cast on (and pick up) for a 16" pillow.

Each of these pillows is constructed of four right-angle triangles. Distinctly different effects can be achieved by varying the colors and/or striping pattern.

BRYSPUN Kid-n-Ewe for each pillow: 1 skein each color 110 (MC) and as CC, color 630 (solid-colored pillow), color 190 (striped pillow), or color 490 (checked pillow)

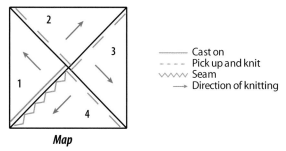

Map

———— Cast on
- - - - Pick up and knit
vvvvv Seam
→ Direction of knitting

equilateral + other triangles

equilateral ╋ other triangles

KNITTING AN EQUILATERAL TRIANGLE

Another triangle that is easy to knit and lends itself to many design possibilities is the equilateral triangle: all three sides of the triangle are the same length and the angles are all 60°. To knit one, cast on the number of stitches for the base (an odd number works best). For garter stitch, work the decreases at each end of every fourth row.

For example, cast on 15 stitches (Row 1) and knit back across the wrong side (Row 2) to form a garter ridge.
• Then decrease 1 stitch in from each edge on every 4th row (k1, ssk, knit to 3 stitches from the end of the row, k2tog, k1).
• When 5 stitches remain, work the decreases on the edge (rather than 1 stitch in from the edge: ssk, k1, k2tog).
• When 3 stitches remain, work a centered 3-to-1 decrease (S2KP2, see page 117) on the right side, then turn and knit the remaining stitch. Cut the yarn and pull it through the loop.

Equilateral triangles can also be knit in other stitch patterns. To knit this triangle in stockinette stitch, decrease 1 stitch in from each edge on every right-side row.

For stitch patterns other than stockinette or garter stitch, you will need to determine the correct decrease ratio. Decide whether the gauge of your chosen stitch pattern is closer to stockinette or to garter stitch. Work a sample triangle using the decrease ratio that corresponds to your estimated gauge. When the triangle is finished, measure the base and the two sides to see if they are all equal. If not, change the decrease frequency: if the triangle is too tall, decrease more often; if it is too short, the decrease rows should be more widely spaced.

BUILDING WITH TRIANGLES

Since all three sides of the equilateral triangle are the same length, you can pick up the number of stitches that were cast on for the first triangle along any side. If you continue to pick up stitches and knit a triangle on the left edge of the triangle just completed, after 6 triangles you will have a neat hexagon.

The hexagon is a versatile motif. It could form the top of a tam, a pillow top, a hot pad or table mat, or one side of a bag. Or, it could combine with similar units to create a larger fabric. Hexagons combined with other units (not necessarily triangles) and/or straight knitting, create all sorts of wondrous designs. More about this later.

It's easy to knit equilateral triangles into strips. After knitting one triangle, pick up stitches along the left edge and knit another. When this second triangle is completed, pick up stitches along the right edge of the second triangle and knit another. Continue this process of alternating the edge where the stitches are picked up and you'll have a strip of equilateral triangles. Add interest by knitting stripes, using hand-dyed yarns, or incorporating different stitches, colors, and/or textures.

An equilateral triangle

In garter, decrease at each end of every 4th row, beginning with the very first row of knitting

In stockinette, decrease at each end of every other row

Build a hexagon with 6 triangles

Build a strip

Combine large and small triangles

Ever-larger triangles

Irregular triangles

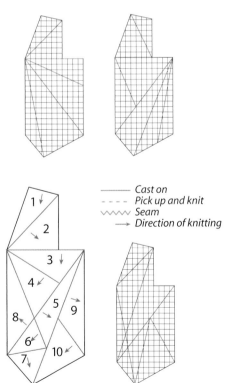

Cast on
Pick up and knit
Seam
Direction of knitting

Building a vest with irregular triangles...
or planning the shapes on graph paper.

VARIATIONS

One way to vary the basic triangle motif is to work with two sizes of triangles, one twice the size of the other. The side of the large triangle is double that of the smaller one, leading to many interesting variations. Another method is to randomly knit equilateral triangles, sometimes picking up twice the base number of stitches and knitting a large triangle. Filling the 'canvas' of a sweater with equilateral triangles works well. Knit them randomly until you have a fairly large piece, then control the size and shape to complete the outline.

Another intriguing method for combining equilateral triangles was suggested in a book published in 1988, *The Knitting Design Book*, by Ank Bredewold and Anneke Pleiter. Their technique begins with 3 small triangles in a strip (numbered 1–3 on our drawing). Then stitches are picked up along the edges of 2 of these triangles and another, twice-as-large triangle is knit (4). Stitches for a second larger triangle are picked up along triangle 4. Each succeeding triangle grows larger (5).

IRREGULAR TRIANGLES

So far, I've discussed carefully controlled triangle shapes— right-angle and equilateral units. But if you like playing and experimenting, you can knit all sorts of irregularly shaped triangles. The decrease ratios can be different on each edge. You can even decrease on one edge and increase on the other (but remember that you must decrease more rapidly than you increase, or you will never reach the point of your triangle!). You can knit individual triangles, lay them out in various arrangements until you find a design that pleases you and then join them together, or you can knit one triangle, pick up stitches anywhere along one of its edges and knit another. Continue to play in this manner, filling in empty spaces as your piece grows. Triangles can be bound off before they're finished, resulting in even more interesting shapes.

To plan your irregular triangles, draw the outline of your fabric or garment on graph paper (or with a computer program that provides grids). Use regular graph paper, 4 or 5 squares per inch, where each square equals an inch. Use a pencil to fill the outline with triangles. When you arrive at an arrangement that is pleasing to you, stop and analyze how it could be knit. Because the design was drawn out on graph paper, you now have a carefully charted outline for each of your triangles. Choose a starting point and count the number of squares on one edge of your starting triangle. Multiply that number by your stitch gauge to determine the number of stitches to cast on. Analyze each triangle individually to determine your cast-on and frequency of decreases.

While many approaches to making this vest are possible (knit each triangle in a different color, use a single color and various textured yarns, combine multiple stitch patterns, or employ subtle striping in each of the triangles), even a single color worked in garter ridge stitch will emphasize the direction of knitting in each triangle.

THE PATTERNS

Two patterns are included here to get you started using equilateral triangles in your knitting. In Adagio, page 40, a simple strip of triangles forms a luxurious scarf. In Hot Summer Nights, page 38, strips form a short-sleeved summer pullover.

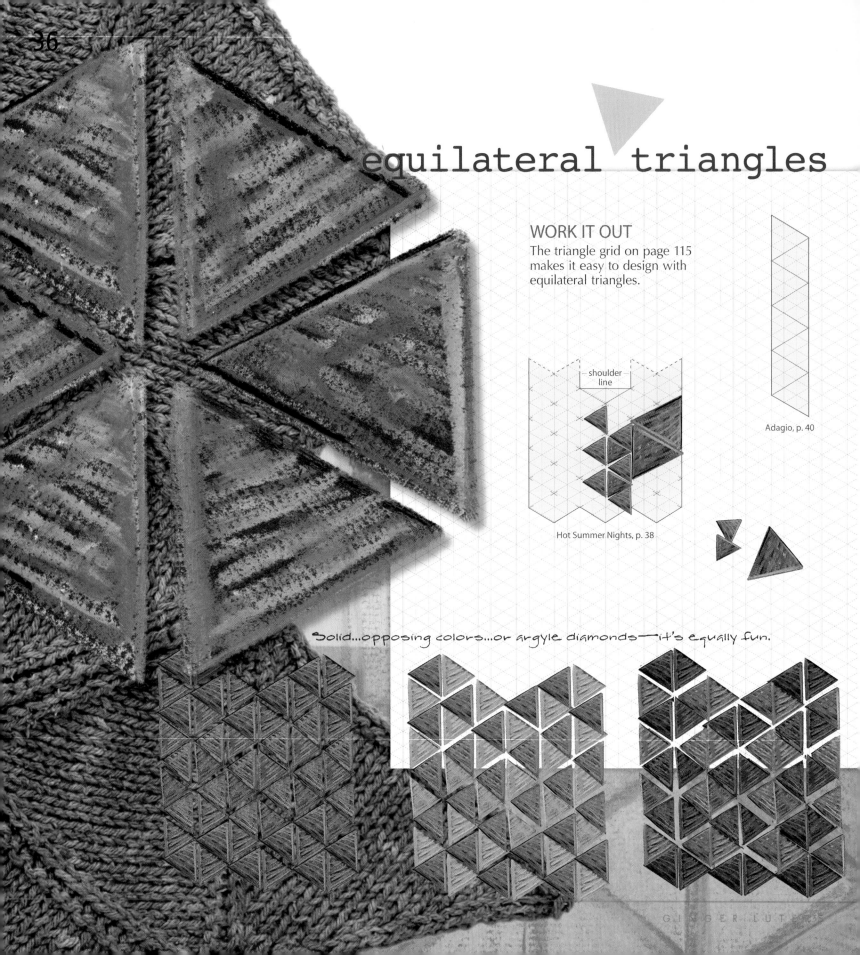

equilateral triangles

WORK IT OUT
The triangle grid on page 115 makes it easy to design with equilateral triangles.

shoulder line

Hot Summer Nights, p. 38

Adagio, p. 40

Solid...opposing colors...or argyle diamonds—it's equally fun.

Equilaterals fall in line.

There's strength
in numbers—
build a hexagon,
a hat, a honeycomb.

SWATCH TRICKS

Turn handpaints loose, or
gain control. Just watch the
colors flow.

Hot Summer Nights

Intermediate

OVERSIZED FIT

S (M, L)

Measures approximately
A *42 (45, 48)"*
B *20 (22½, 25)"*
C *10½ (11¼, 12)"*

10cm/4"

28 | GET GAUGE!
20

*over stockinette stitch
(knit on RS, purl on WS)*

1 2 3 **4** 5 6

Medium weight
MC *1800 (2035, 2285) yds*
CC *560 (635, 710) yds*

*4.5mm/US 7
or size to obtain gauge*

Size G

*1 spare circular needle
of required size for
3-needle bind-off*

NOTES

1 See *Techniques*, page 116, for 3-needle bind-off, ssk, S2KP2, ssp, and single crochet (sc). **2** In these instructions, "pick up" means "pick up and knit." Pick up all stitches with RS facing. **3** Refer to Map for placement of Basic Triangles and direction of work. Shading on Map indicates a Modified Basic Triangle; see additional instructions. **4** Vertical Strips of triangles are knit, then joined with 3-needle bind-off.

BASIC TRIANGLE

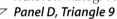

Row 1 (RS) With CC, cast on (or pick up, depending on where you are on the Map) 21 (23, 25) sts.
Row 2 Knit.
Row 3 Change to MC, k1, ssk, knit to last 3 sts, k2tog, k1.
Row 4 Purl.
Repeat Rows 3 and 4 until 5 sts remain.
Next RS row K1, S2KP2, k1.
Next row Purl.
Next row S2KP2. Fasten off. Basic Triangle measures 4 (4½, 5)" along a side when joined to other triangles; a strip of Basic Triangles measures approximately 3½ (3¾, 4)" wide when joined to other strips.

BACK

Beginning with Triangle 1, and following the numbers on the Map, work Basic Triangles (unshaded blocks) and work shaded blocks as follows:

Panel C, Triangle 9
With CC, pick up 21 (23, 25) sts.
Knit 1 row.
Next row (RS) K1, ssk, knit to last 3 sts, k2tog, k1.
Next row (WS) P1, p2tog, purl to end.
Repeat last 2 rows until 2 sts remain.
Next row K2tog. Fasten off.

Panel D, Triangle 9
Work as Panel C, reversing shaping on WS row (p to last 3 sts, p2tog, p1).

FRONT

Beginning with Triangle 1 and following the numbers on the Map, work Basic Triangles.

FINISHING

Block each Panel. Arrange the Strips according to the Maps.
With CC, pick up sts along the long edge of Back Panel A, picking up 21 (23, 25) sts along each Triangle—105 (115, 125) sts. With separate needle, pick up the same number of sts along the long edge of Back Panel B. Join these two Strips using 3-needle bind-off.
Join all Back Strips and Front Strips using this technique, picking up 11 (11, 12) sts along shaded Triangle 9.

Shoulder seams
With CC, pick up 21 (23, 25) sts along top of Triangle 9 on Back Panel A. Knit 1 row, bind off. Repeat for Strips B, E, and F. Sew the top edge of Triangle 10 on Front Strips A and B to the edge just bound off on Back Strips E and F. Repeat for the other shoulder seam.

Side seams
Join Front to Back at each side seam, using CC and 3-needle bind-off, leaving top 7½ (8, 8)" open for armhole.

Crochet edge
With crochet hook and CC, work 1 row single crochet (sc) along bottom edge, working a decrease (skipping a st) at inner corners and an increase (working 2 sc into one st) at outer points.
Work 2 rows sc around each armhole, working 4 evenly spaced decreases in second row.
Work 2 rows sc around neck edge, working decreases in inner corners and at neck center front. Sew in ends and block lightly.

Vertical strips of equilateral triangles are knit in a luscious, handpainted yarn, then outlined with a darker tone.

Module Size

	S	M	L
Inches	4	4½	5
Stitches	21	23	25
Strip Width	3½	3¾	4

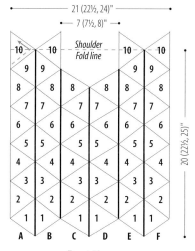

Front Map

— Cast on
- - - Pick up and knit
⋁⋁⋀⋀ Seam
→ Direction of knitting
━━ 3-needle bind-off

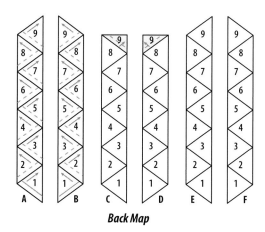

Back Map

CHERRY TREE HILL Silk and Merino DK 3 skeins Wild Cherry (MC); 1 skein Silk Bouclé Plum (CC); shown in Medium

Adagio

NOTES

1 See *Techniques*, page 116, for ssk, S2KP2, and sewn bind-off. **2** In these instructions, "pick up" means "pick up and knit." Pick up stitches with RS facing and into the edge stitch rather than one stitch in from the edge. **3** Refer to Map for placement of Basic Triangles and direction of work.

BASIC TRIANGLE

Row 1 (RS) With B, cast on (or pick up, depending on where you are on the Map) 45 sts.
Row 2 Knit.
Row 3 With MC, k1, ssk, knit to last 3 sts, k2tog, k1.
Row 4 Knit.
Rows 5, 6 With A, knit.
Repeat Rows 3–6 until 5 sts remain.
Next RS row K1, S2KP2, k1.
Next row Knit.
Next 2 rows With A, knit.
Next row (RS) S2KP2. Fasten off. Basic Triangle measures approximately 9½" when joined to other triangles.

Scarf

Triangle 1
Work Basic Triangle.

Triangles 2–8
With B, pick up 45 sts as shown on Map. Work Basic Triangle, beginning with Row 2 instructions. Finish the right edge of Triangle 8 by picking up 45 sts with B, knit 1 row. Bind off with sewn bind-off.

Trim

With B, pick up sts along one long edge of scarf, picking up 43 sts along each Triangle—172 sts. Knit 1 row. Bind off with sewn bind-off. Repeat for other long edge.

FINISHING

Block lightly and weave in ends, weaving each end into its appropriate color area so that the wrong side of the scarf looks neat.

———— Cast on
– – – – Pick up and knit
——→ Direction of knitting

Module Size

Inches	9½
Stitches	45

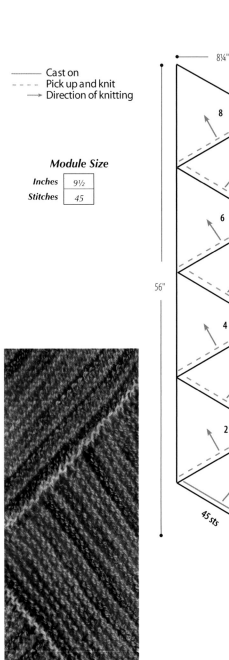

CHERRY TREE HILL *Suri Lace Weight Alpaca Wild Cherry (MC), Burgandy (A), and Peach (B)*

mitered squares

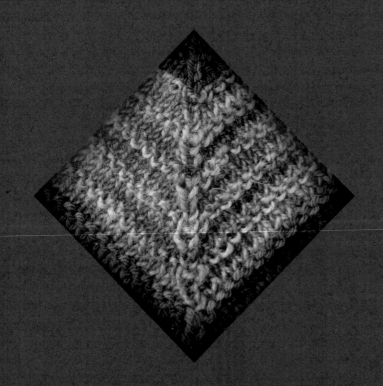

mitered squares

What is a knitted mitered square? It's a square of knitting with stitches set at right angles to each other. A diagonal dividing line formed by decreases reaches across from one corner to the other. To me, these squares are magic! They are such fun to create, and they provide seemingly unlimited design possibilities.

Knitting a mitered square

KNITTING A MITERED SQUARE

To knit a mitered square, first decide on the size of the square you want to knit, then cast on enough stitches to make two sides of that square. Knit back and forth across these stitches, decreasing in the center of the row. These center decreases pull the knitting in and form a miter (diagonal) line through the center of the piece of knitting. To complete the square, simply continue knitting and decreasing until there are no more stitches.

The only trick here is to figure the correct frequency of decreases to form a square. Fortunately, there are some guidelines that help in this process. In garter stitch or stitch patterns with a similar stitch-to-row ratio, work 2 decreases in the center of the row on every other row (over 4 rows, 4 stitches are decreased). I prefer to decrease on right-side rows. For stockinette stitch, the ratio is 2 decreases in 3 of every 4 rows (over 4 rows of knitting, 6 stitches are decreased).

I'll discuss the knitting details in a moment, but first let me tell you how I became so fascinated with these little squares.

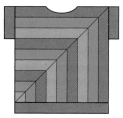

One big mitered square

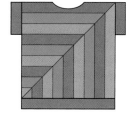

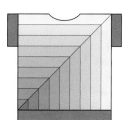

Play with stripes and colors

SOLVING A PUZZLE

Several years ago, when I was first designing knitwear, I saw a sweater in a small shop in southern California that had vertical and horizontal stripes. I went home and thought about how it was made. After a few experiments, I tried casting on enough stitches for the top and left side of this basically square sweater front, and then worked back and forth in stockinette stitch. I put a marker in the center of the row of stitches and worked a decrease before and after the marker. I knew that knit stitches weren't square, but I wasn't certain as to how frequently to decrease in order to end up with a square. More trial and error followed until I found that if I worked the decreases in 3 of every 4 rows, I ended up with a square.

I designed quite a few sweaters using this basic idea of one big mitered square, playing with stripes and colors. Then I found that I didn't have to knit squares. I could cast on more stitches before or after the center marker and knit rectangles!

Lengthen one side

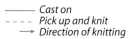

——— Cast on
- - - - Pick up and knit
——→ Direction of knitting

BUILDING WITH MITERED SQUARES

This discovery led to more designs and soon I was experimenting again. I wondered, 'What if I don't want the entire sweater front to be just one big square?' I could knit several smaller squares and join them together. The idea of sewing many small squares together wasn't too appealing, but I soon realized I could pick up stitches along one side of a square, and then cast on more stitches, to have enough for the two sides of the next square.

Building with mitered squares: Pick up stitches along one side of the first square and cast on for second side of the next square

Paired decreases

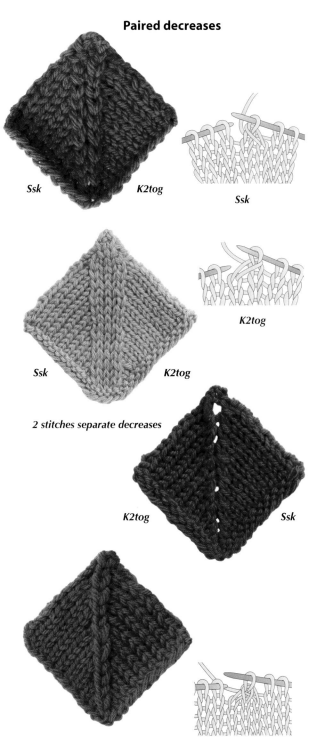

Ssk   K2tog

Ssk

K2tog

Ssk   K2tog

2 stitches separate decreases

K2tog   Ssk

Centered double decrease

More experimenting and designing followed. This was before computers entered my life, and certainly before I thought of using a computer as a design tool. So I drew the sweaters on graph paper, erased, and drew some more. Sometime in the midst of all this experimentation, one of my students gave me a copy of a book published in 1952, Number Knitting, by Virginia Woods Bellamy. What a surprise! This innovative knitter had been following this same path and, working primarily in garter stitch, had knitted mitered squares all those many years earlier. If you get a chance to take a look at this long out-of-print book, don't miss it.

TYPES OF DECREASES

Now, back to the actual knitting of mitered squares. There are many ways to work the decreases, each of which gives a slightly different appearance to the overall garment or knit fabric. Some methods emphasize the decrease line, while others make it less obvious. Let's take a look at a few of these techniques. You might want to knit a small sample of each, remembering that decreases are worked every other row in garter stitch and in 3 of every 4 rows in stockinette stitch. The swatches show the various decrease methods worked in stockinette stitch so that the decrease line is more prominent, but the instructions are for working mitered squares in garter stitch.

PAIRED DECREASES

This method tends to de-emphasize the decrease line. Right-slanting (k2tog) and left-slanting (ssk) decreases are used in this technique. The order in which you work them is a matter of personal choice, but be consistent, as each has a slightly different appearance.
Row 1 Cast on enough stitches for one side of the square (for example, 15 stitches), place a marker on your needle and cast on the stitches for the other side of the square (another 15 stitches).
Row 2 (WS) Knit.
Row 3 Knit to 2 stitches before the marker, k2tog, slip marker to right needle, ssk, knit to the end of the row.
Row 4 Knit.
Repeat Rows 3 and 4 until 2 stitches remain. K2tog and pull yarn through the loop.

This is probably the simplest of the decrease methods, and while it isn't really my favorite, there are some situations in which it's useful. You can vary the appearance by moving the decreases one or two stitches away from the center marker.

CENTERED DOUBLE DECREASE

This method emphasizes the decrease line with what looks like a row of slip stitches along the diagonal centerline. It is the one I use most often. In this technique, both decreases are worked in one operation.
Row 1 Cast on enough stitches for one side of the square (15 stitches), one stitch for the centerline, and 15 stitches for the other side of the square (31 stitches total). I don't use a marker for this technique; I think it's more trouble than it's worth, since the decrease line becomes visible after a couple of decreases have been worked.
Row 2 (WS) Knit all stitches except the center stitch, which is purled.

mitered squares

Row 3 Knit to 1 stitch before the center stitch (knit 14 stitches in this example), work an S2KP2 decrease, and then knit to the end of the row.
Row 4 Knit all stitches except the center stitch, which is purled.
Repeat Rows 3 and 4 until one stitch remains. Cut yarn and pull it through the loop.

DOUBLE DECREASES ON WRONG-SIDE ROWS

This is the method preferred by Horst Schulz and is shown in his wonderful books, Patchwork Knitting and Fashion for Children. Working in garter stitch or garter ridge stitch, cast on as for the double-decrease method. On wrong-side rows, k3tog when you reach the center 3 stitches.

Remember that these examples involve garter stitch or garter ridge stitch. In stockinette stitch, work the decreases in 3 of every 4 rows. This means that some decreases will be worked on wrong-side rows, so you'll need to do the purl version of whatever decrease you've chosen.

VARIATIONS

Once you understand the basic construction of these squares, then the real fun begins! There are many ways to change their appearance in the construction. One of the easiest is to add stripes. Stripes are particularly effective because they emphasize the multidirectional nature of the knitting. I like to knit 2-row stripes in the garter ridge pattern, using the double-decrease method. Hand-dyed or variegated yarns are also effective. If you use other stitch or color patterns, such as seed stitch, Fair Isle, or slip-stitch patterns, be aware that your stitch and row gauges may change, in which case you may need to adjust the decrease frequency.

You can also arrange the squares in many different ways to achieve interesting visual effects. For example, the squares can be aligned in the same direction. This gives a nice orderliness to the pattern. Or, the diagonals can be placed in random directions.

Rotating the squares by 45° can produce a diamond pattern. As with other square arrangements, the effect can be subtle (in a single handpainted yarn), or dramatic (when enhanced with black outlines).

4-SQUARE SQUARE

Can you see how the swatch on page 47 was knit? The first square is striped to emphasize the mitered lines. Square 2 is knit by casting on stitches for one side of the square plus one center stitch, and then picking up stitches for the other side of the square along the edge of Square 1. From these stitches another square is knit. The process is repeated for Squares 3 and 4. These four small squares form one larger square. Rotating this larger square by 45° can produce even more complex-looking patterns.

Another interesting pattern is created by knitting a panel of striped mitered squares with the diagonals aligned in the same direction. The next panel is knit using the same technique, but starting from the opposite end of the panel.

Double decrease on wrong-side row

Garter ridge stripes   *Use hand-dyed yarns*

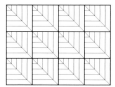

Align the miters

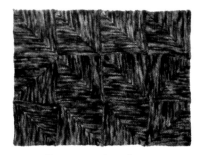

Or arrange at random

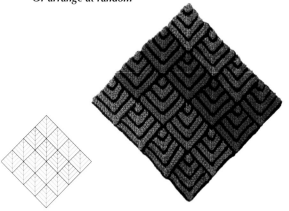

Rotate for a diamond

A 4-square motif

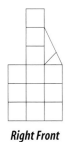

—————— *Cast on*
- - - - *Pick up and knit*
——→ *Direction of knitting*

The outline of a mitered square vest pattern is the type of pattern that I often spend hours playing with on my computer. I draw the lines of the miters in various directions until I achieve a pleasing design. Sometimes only part of the vest is composed of miters; other parts might be a solid color or knit in other stitch patterns.

PATTERNS
Times Square, pages 50–53, and Yuba River, pages 54–55, are based on simple mitered squares, one with a combination of stripes and solid areas and the other with stripes throughout each square.

4-square motifs joined and rotated

3-squares and 4-squares

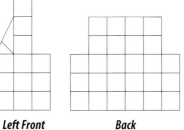 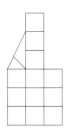

Right Front   **Left Front**   **Back**

Plan a mitered vest

Alternate diagonals

mitered squares

Yuba River, p. 54

Times Square, p.50

WORK IT OUT

Use the grid on page 114 to create squares or diamonds. Arrange blocks, add colors, start knitting.

Diamonds
built diagonally.
It's so easy.

Complete a mitered
square with a solid
colored block

SWATCH TRICKS

Garter Ridge Pattern is
perfect for fancy yarns.
A touch of glitz, a bit of
shine—a lot of effect.

Times Square

NOTES

1 See *Techniques*, page 116, for Make 1 (M1), ssk, p2tog, S2KP2, loop cast-on, wrap and turn (W&T) and hiding wraps. **2** In these instructions, "pick up" means "pick up and knit." Pick up all stitches with RS facing and MC. **3** Refer to Map for placement of Mitered Squares and direction of work. **4** When casting on AND picking up sts for a Mitered Square, cast on the corner st. **5** Sleeves are knit from side to side. **6** Yarn is used doubled throughout pattern.

GARTER RIDGE PATTERN

Rows 1, 3 (RS) Knit.
Row 2 Knit.
Row 4 Purl.
Repeat Rows 1–4 for Garter Ridge Pattern.

RIGHT MITERED SQUARE

Row 1 With MC, cast on (or pick up, depending on where you are on the Map) 29 (31, 33) sts— 14+1+14 (15+1+15, 16+1+16).
Row 2 (WS) Knit.
Row 3 With A, knit to 1 st before the center (corner) st, S2KP2, knit to end.
Row 4 Purl.
Row 5 With MC, work Row 3.
Row 6 Knit to the corner st, p1, knit to end.
Rows 7–14 Work Rows 3–6 twice, EXCEPT on Row 14, instead of purling the corner st, p2tog (the corner st and the next st).
Row 15 With B, k7 (8, 9), p2tog tbl, turn work.
Row 16 Purl.
Row 17 K7 (8, 9), p2tog tbl, turn work.
Row 18 Knit.
Rows 19–28 (19–30, 19–32) [Work Rows 15–18] 2 (3, 3) times, then [work Rows 15, 16] 1 (0, 1) time. Bind off, working p2tog tbl as usual. Mitered Square measures approximately 3 (3¼, 3½)" when joined to other squares.

RIGHT MITERED HALF-SQUARE

Row 1 Pick up 14 (15, 16) sts along previous square, cast on corner st, pick up 6 (7, 8) sts along Panel. Beginning with Row 2, work as Right Mitered Square through Row 12 (14, 16).
With MC (MC, B), bind off, working S2KP2 (k2tog, k2tog) on last 3 (2, 2) sts.

LEFT MITERED SQUARE

Work as Right Mitered Square through Row 13.
Row 14 Knit.
Row 15 With B, k7 (8, 9), k2tog, knit to end.
Row 16 P7 (8, 9), p2tog, turn work.
Row 17 Knit.
Row 18 K7 (8, 9), p2tog, turn work.
Row 19 Knit.
Rows 20–27 (20–28, 20–31) [Work Rows 16–19] 2 (2, 3) times, then [work Rows 16 and 17] 0 (1, 0) time. Bind off purlwise (knitwise, purlwise), working p2tog (k2tog, p2tog) as usual.

LEFT MITERED HALF-SQUARE

Row 1 Pick up 6 (7, 8) sts along Panel, cast on corner st, pick up 14 (15, 16) sts along square. Continue as for Left Mitered Square through Row 12 (14, 14).
Size S: Bind off, working S2KP2 as usual.
Size M: With MC, S2KP2, on first 3 sts as beginning of bind-off and continue bind-off across row.
Size L: Row 15 With B, k1, k2tog, k9.
Row 16 P9, p2tog.
Bind off.

RIGHT HALF OF JACKET (BACK AND FRONT)

Note Use larger needles throughout.
Beginning with Panel A, then Square 1, and following the numbers on the Map, work Right Mitered Squares (unshaded blocks) and shaded Squares and Panels as follows:

Panel A
Row 1 With MC, cast on 76 (82, 88) sts.
Row 2 (WS) Knit.
Short Rows 3, 4 K75, wrap and turn (W&T), purl to end.
Short Rows 5, 6 K45, W&T, purl to end.
Row 7 Knit, hiding wraps.
Row 8 Purl.
Short Rows 9, 10 K30, W&T, purl to end.
Short Rows 11, 12 K60, W&T, purl to end.
Rows 13, 14 Knit.
Bind off.
Work Squares 1–5.
Square 6
Work Right Mitered Half-Square.
Panel B
With MC, pick up 76 (82, 88) sts along Squares 1–6, then cast on 8 sts—84 (90, 96) sts.

This striking jacket is constructed of panels of striped mitered squares that are completed with small squares of solid red. These panels are joined to the bands of solid black as you knit, so there is very little sewing involved. The black bands are wider at the bottom than at the top, which provides a flattering swing line to the jacket.

Work as Panel A, beginning with Row 2.
Work Squares 7–12.

Panel C
With MC, pick up 84 (90, 96) sts. Work as Panel A, beginning with Row 2.
Work squares 13–15.

Square 16
Work Right Mitered Half-Square.

Panel D
Row 1 With MC, pick up 48 (52, 56) sts along Squares 13–16.
Row 2 Knit.
Short Rows 3, 4 K45, W&T, purl to end.
Short Rows 5, 6 K30, W&T, purl to end.
Row 7 Knit.
Row 8 Purl.
Short Rows 9, 10 K15, W&T, purl to end.
Short Rows 11, 12 K40, W&T, purl to end.
Rows 13, 14 Knit.
Bind off.
Work Squares 17–19.

Square 20
Work Right Mitered Half-Square.

Panel E
With MC, pick up 48 (52, 56) sts, along Squares 17–20, then cast on 36 (38, 40) sts—84 (90, 96) sts. Work as Panel A, beginning with Row 2.
Work Squares 21–26.

Panel F
Work as Panel C.
Work Squares 27–29.

Square 30
Work as Basic Right Mitered Square EXCEPT begin **Rows 3 and 9**, k1, k2tog and work remaining rows as follows:
Row 15 K1, k2tog, k2 (3, 4), k2tog.
Row 16 Purl.
Row 17 K4 (5, 6), k2tog.
Row 18 Knit.
Row 19 K4 (5, 6), k2tog.
Row 20 Purl.
Row 21 K1, k2tog, k1 (2, 3), k2tog.
Row 22 Knit.
Row 23 K3 (4, 5), k2tog.
Row 24 Purl.
Row 25 K1, k2tog, k0 (1, 2), k2tog.
Row 26 Knit.
Row 27 K2 (3, 4), k2tog.
Size S Bind off, working k2tog as usual.

LUCCI YARNS Cravenella 6 (8, 8) balls Black (MC); 3 (4, 4) balls Putty (A); 2 (2, 2) balls Scarlet (B); shown in Medium

Row 29 K2 (3), k2tog.
Row 30 Knit.
Size M Bind off, working k2tog as usual.
Row 29 K2, k2tog.
Row 30 Purl.
Size L Bind off, working ssk as usual.

Square 31
With MC, pick up 9 (10, 11) sts across Square 30, cast on corner st, pick up 14 (15, 16) sts along Panel F. Beginning with Row 2, work through Row 12 (14, 14) of Basic Right Mitered Square, EXCEPT *Size L* begin Row 3 with k1, k2tog; *All Sizes* begin Rows 9 and 11 with k1, k2tog; *Sizes M, L* begin Row 14 with k9, p1, k2. With MC, bind off, working S2KP2 as usual. Leave last st on needle.

Square 32
Row 1 With MC, pick up 6 (7, 8) sts across Square 31, cast on corner st, pick up 7 sts along Panel F.
Row 2 Knit to last 2 sts, k2tog.
Row 3 With A, k1, k2tog, k2 (3, 3), S2KP2, k3, ssk, k1.
Row 4 Purl.
Row 5 With MC, k1, k2tog, k0 (1, 1), S2KP2, k1, ssk, k1.
Row 6 K3, p1, k2 (k2tog, k2tog), k0 (1, 1).
Bind off, working S2KP2 as usual.

Module Size			
	S	M	L
Inches	3	3¼	3½
Stitches	14+1+14	15+1+15	16+1+16

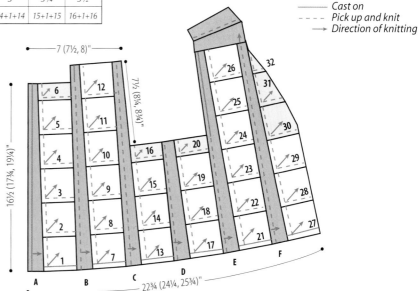

Cast on
Pick up and knit
Direction of knitting

Right Front and Back Map

Times Square

LEFT HALF OF JACKET (BACK AND FRONT)

Note It may be helpful to mark every 14 (15, 16)th st from bottom of Panels before picking up sts for Squares.

Square 33
With MC, beginning along cast-on edge of Panel A, and 14 (15, 16) sts above lower edge, pick up 14 (15, 16) sts down Panel A to edge, then cast on 15 (16, 17) sts. Work Left Mitered Square, beginning with Row 2. Work Squares 34–37.

Square 38
Work Left Mitered Half-Square.

Panel G
Row 1 With MC, cast on 8 sts, then pick up 76 (82, 88) sts along Squares 38–33—84 (90, 96) sts.
Row 2 (WS) Knit.
Row 3 Knit.
Short Rows 4, 5 P60, W&T, knit to end.
Short Rows 6, 7 P30, W&T, knit to end.
Row 8 Purl.
Row 9 Knit.
Short Rows 10, 11 P45, knit to end.
Short Rows 12, 13 P75, knit to end.
Row 14 Knit. Bind off.
Work Squares 39–44.

Panel H
With MC, pick up 84 (90, 96) sts.
Row 2 (WS) Knit.
Short Rows 3, 4 K60, W&T, purl to end.
Short Rows 5, 6 K30, W&T, purl to end.
Row 7 Knit, hiding wraps.
Row 8 Purl.
Short Rows 9, 10 K45, W&T, purl to end.
Short Rows 11, 12 K75, W&T, purl to end.
Rows 13, 14 Knit.
Bind off.
Work Squares 45–47.

Square 48
Work Left Mitered Half-Square.

Panel I
Row 1 With MC, pick up 48 (52, 56) sts along Squares 45–48.
Row 2 Knit.
Short Rows 3, 4 K40, W&T, purl to end.
Short Rows 5, 6 K15, W&T, purl to end.
Row 7 Knit.
Row 8 Purl.
Short Rows 9, 10 K30, W&T, purl to end.
Short Rows 11, 12 K45, W&T, purl to end.

Rows 13, 14 Knit.
Bind off.
Work Squares 49–51.

Square 52
Work Left Mitered Half-Square.

Panel J
With MC, pick up 48 (52, 56) sts along Squares 49–52, then cast on 36 (38, 40) sts—84 (90, 96 sts).
Work as Panel H, starting with Row 2.
Work Squares 53–58.

Panel K
Work as Panel H.
Work Squares 59–61.

Square 62
Work as Left Mitered Square through Row 13 EXCEPT, end Rows 3 and 9 ssk, k1.
Row 14 K5 (6, 7), p2tog, knit to end.
Row 15 With B, k7 (8, 9), k2tog, k2 (3, 4), ssk, k1.
Row 16 P4 (5, 6), p2tog.
Row 17 Knit.
Row 18 K4 (5, 6), k2tog.
Row 19 Knit.
Row 20 P4 (5, 6), p2tog.
Row 21 K2 (3, 4), ssk, k1.
Row 22 K3 (4, 5), k2tog.
Row 23 Knit.
Row 24 P3 (4, 5), p2tog.
Row 25 K1 (2, 3), ssk, k1.
Row 26 K2 (3, 4), k2tog.
Row 27 Knit.
Size S Bind off, working last 2 sts as p2tog.
Row 28 P2 (3), p2tog.
Row 29 Knit.
Size M Bind off knitwise, working last 2 sts as k2tog.
Row 30 K2, k2tog.
Row 31 Knit.
Bind off, working last 2 sts as p2tog.

Square 63
Row 1 With MC, pick up 14 (15, 16) sts along Panel K, cast on corner st, pick up 9 (10, 11) sts along Square 62. Beginning with Row 2, work Left Mitered Square through Row 12 (14, 14) EXCEPT *Size S*, end Rows 9 and 11 as ssk, k1; *Size M*, end Rows 9 and 11 as ssk, k1 and work Row 14 as k2, p1, k9; for *Size L*, end Rows 3, 9 and 11 as ssk, k1 and work Row 14 as k2, p1, k9. Bind off with MC, working S2KP2 as usual.

Square 64
Row 1 With MC, pick up 7 sts along Panel K, cast on corner st, pick up 6 (7, 7) sts along Square 63.
Row 2 Knit.

Row 3 With A, k1, k2tog, k3, S2KP2, k2 (3, 3), ssk, k1.
Row 4 Purl.
Row 5 With MC, k1, k2tog, k1, S2KP2, k0 (1, 1), ssk, k1.
Row 6 K2 (1, 1), k0 (k2tog, k2tog), p1, k3.
Bind off, working S2KP2 as usual.

Left shoulder

With MC, pick up 19 (20, 21) sts across Panel G, Square 44, and Panel H.
Row 2 (WS) Knit.
Short Rows 3, 4 K17, W&T, purl to end.
Short Rows 5, 6 K14, W&T, knit to end.
Short Rows 7, 8 K11, W&T, purl to end.
Short Rows 9, 10 K8, W&T, knit to end.
Short Rows 11, 12 K5, W&T, purl to end.
Short Rows 13, 14 K3, W&T, knit to end.
Row 15 Knit.
Row 16 Purl.
Reverse short-row shaping by working Rows 13, 14, then 11, 12, etc., end with Rows 3, 4. Knit 2 rows. Bind off. Sew to Left Front.

Right shoulder

With MC, pick up 19 (20, 21) sts across Panel F, Square 26, and Panel E. Work as for Left shoulder. Sew to Right Back.

SLEEVES

The Sleeves are knit in Garter Ridge Pattern, alternating 2 rows MC and 2 rows A.
Row 1 With MC and larger needle, cast on 31 (34, 38) sts.
Row 2 (WS) Knit.
Short Rows 3, 4 K14 (15, 16), W&T, purl to end.
Short Rows 5, 6 K18 (19, 21), W&T, knit to end.
Short Rows 7, 8 K22 (23, 26), W&T, purl to end.
Short Rows 9, 10 K26 (28, 31), W&T, knit to end.
Short Rows 11, 12 K30 (33, 37), W&T, purl to end.
Work 122 (126, 130) rows Garter Ridge Pattern over all sts. Reverse short-row shaping, beginning with Short Rows 11, 12 and ending with Short Rows 3, 4. Knit 2 rows.
Bind off.

Cuff

Row 1 With larger needle, pick up 65 (67, 69) sts along short edge of Sleeve.
Row 2 Knit.
Rows 3, 4 Change to smaller needle and knit.
Rows 5, 6 With A, knit.
Rows 7, 8 With MC, knit.
Row 9 With B, knit.
Bind off.

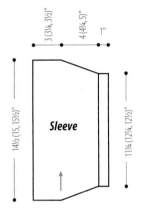

Sleeve

—— Cast on
---- Pick up and knit
→ Direction of knitting

FINISHING

Sew top of sleeves to armhole, sewing straight part of Sleeve sides to underarm edge. Sew Sleeve seams.

Jacket Bottom Edging

Row 1 With circular needle, pick up 246 (260, 274) sts along bottom of jacket. Work as Cuff, beginning with Row 2.

FRONT AND NECK BAND

Row 1 With circular needle, beginning at lower Right Front corner, pick up 47 (50, 53) sts along Right Front to beginning of neck shaping, place marker (pm), 51 (54, 57) sts to top center of shoulder, 58 (60, 62) sts to center of left shoulder, 51 (54, 57) sts along left neck edge, pm, and 47 (50, 53) sts down Left Front—254 (268, 282) sts.
Row 2 Knit.
Row 3 Knit, M1, before first marker and after second marker.
Row 4 Knit.
Rows 5 and 6 With A, knit.
Row 7 (Buttonhole row) With MC, k3, yo, k2tog, * k8 (9, 10), yo, k2tog, repeat from * three times more (a total of 5 buttonholes); then knit, M1 st before first marker, working 3 evenly spaced decreases (k2tog) across back neck, and M1 after second marker.
Row 8 Knit.
Row 9 With B, knit.
Bind off.
Sew in ends and block lightly. Sew buttons to left front band to match buttonholes.

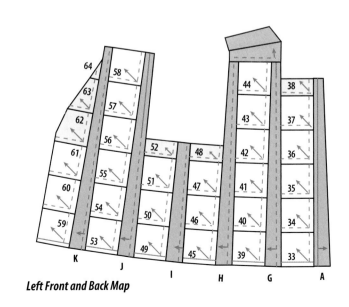

Left Front and Back Map

Yuba River

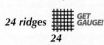

NOTES

1 See *Techniques*, page 116, for ssk, Make 1 (M1), single crochet (sc), and wrap and turn (W&T). **2** In these instructions, "pick up" means "pick up and knit." Pick up all stitches with RS facing and MC. **3** Refer to Map for placement of Basic Mitered Squares and direction of work. Shading on Map indicates a modified Mitered Square; see additional instructions.

BASIC MITERED SQUARE

Row 1 With MC, cast on (or pick up, depending on where you are on the Map) 15 (16, 17, 18) sts, place marker (pm), cast on or pick up 15 (16, 17, 18) more sts.
Row 2 (WS) Knit.
Row 3 With CC, knit to 2 sts before marker, k2tog, ssk, knit remainder of sts.
Row 4 Knit.
Rows 5, 6 With MC, repeat Rows 3 and 4.
Repeat Rows 3–6 until 2 sts remain and you are ready start a RS row. K2tog, fasten off. Basic Mitered Square measures approximately 2½ (2¾, 3, 3¼)" when joined to other squares.

SWEATER FRONT

Beginning with Square 1 and following the numbers on the Map, work Basic Mitered Squares (unshaded blocks) and work shaded blocks as follows:

Triangles 2, 6, 12, 20, and 30
Row 1 With MC, pick up 15 (16, 17, 18) sts.
Row 2 Knit.
Row 3 (RS) With CC, knit to last 3 sts, k2tog, k1.
Row 4 Knit.
Continue in established pattern (2 rows MC, 2 rows CC), decreasing 1 st every RS row. When 3 sts remain, k2tog, k1.
Next row K2.
Next row K2tog, cut yarn and fasten off.

Triangles 41, 51, 58, 67, and 69
Work as for Basic Mitered Square, EXCEPT work RS rows as follows: K1, ssk, knit to 2 sts before marker, k2tog, ssk, knit to last 3 sts, k2tog, k1.

Triangles 42, 52, 59, 64, and 68
Row 1 With MC, pick up 15 (16, 17, 18) sts.
Row 2 Knit.
Row 3 (RS) With CC, k1, ssk, knit remaining sts.

Row 4 Knit.
Continue in established pattern, decreasing 1 st every RS row.
When 3 sts remain, ssk, k1.
Next row K2.
Next row Ssk, fasten off.

SWEATER BACK

Begining with Square 1 and following the Map, work shaded blocks as follows:
Triangles 70 and 71
Work as Triangle 41.
For the Back Triangle 58 is a full-sized Basic Mitered Square (see detail of Map). Work Squares 1–57 the same as Front.

RIGHT SHOULDER

With MC, pick up 36 (40, 44, 48) sts along Front Triangles 51 and 41.
Knit 1 row.
Front shoulder shaping: Short Rows 1, 2 (RS) K4, wrap next st and turn (W&T), knit to end.
Short Rows 3, 4 K8, W&T, knit to end.
Rows 5–18 Continue, working 4 more sts before W&T each RS row—36 sts (size S complete).
Short Rows 19, 20 K40, W&T, knit to end (size M complete).
Short Rows 21, 22 K44, W&T, knit to end—44 sts (size L complete).
Short Rows 23, 24 K48, W&T, knit to end—48 sts (size 1X complete).
Back shoulder shaping Beginning with k36 (40, 44, 48) sts, and working 4 fewer sts before W&T each RS row, work until last row: K4, W&T, knit to end.
Bind off.

LEFT SHOULDER

Work as Right Shoulder, EXCEPT pick up sts along Back Triangles 51 and 41.
Sew Left Shoulder to Left Front of sweater.

NECKBAND

With MC and smaller needle, pick up 108 (118, 128, 138) sts along neck edge.
Knit 3 rows.
Dec row Knit, spacing 9 (10, 11, 13) k2tog decreases evenly—99 (108, 117, 125) sts.
Knit 3 rows.

This easy-to-knit summer pullover is constructed of two-color garter stitch mitered squares that are turned on their points to create diamond-like shapes.

Dec row Knit, spacing 9 (10, 11, 13) k2tog decreases evenly—90 (98, 106, 112) sts.
Knit 3 rows.
Dec row Knit, spacing 9 (10, 11, 13) k2tog decreases evenly—81 (88, 95, 99) sts.
Next row Knit.
Bind off and sew right shoulder seam.

SLEEVE BANDS

With smaller needle and MC, pick up 54 (58, 62, 68) sts around sleeve edge.
Knit 13 rows.
Bind off.

FINISHING

Block Front and Back sections to desired dimensions. Sew side seams and sew in ends. With MC, work 1 row single crochet (sc) around the bottom edge of sweater, working 2 sc in each lower point and 1 dec in each inner point.

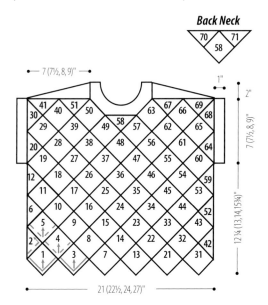

Module Size				
	S	**M**	**L**	**1X**
Inches	2½	2¾	3	3¼
Stitches	15+15	16+16	17+17	18+18
Diagonal Inches	13½	3¾	4½	4½

——— Cast on
- - - - Pick up and knit
——→ Direction of knitting

AURORA YARNS Garnstudio Silke-Tweed 4 (4, 5, 7) skeins in color 24 (MC) and 3 (3, 4, 6) skeins in color 25 (CC); shown in Medium

miters + beyond

miters ✛ beyond

EXPLORE THE POSSIBILITIES

I've talked about the basics of knitting a mitered square and the possibility of rotating these squares to create even more design variations (pages 44–46). With the understanding of this basic concept, there are seemingly countless and very exciting (to me, anyway) opportunities to create interesting color and pattern combinations.

INTARSIA MITERED SQUARES

One simple method that opens up a whole new range of design ideas is to knit each mitered square in two colors, one on each side of the center decrease line. This intarsia technique works best with decreases placed on either side of a center marker.

Let's start working a mitered square using this intarsia technique. To knit one of these squares in garter stitch, cast on the stitches for one side of the square, put a marker on the needle, then cast on the same number of stitches with a second color. Knit back across the wrong side, changing colors at the marker (being certain to pick up the new color from behind the old to prevent a hole, and keeping this twist on the wrong side). On each right-side row, knit to 2 stitches before the marker, k2tog, slip the marker, pick up (and twist) the second color, work an ssk decrease, and finish the row. Repeat these 2 rows until 2 stitches remain, then k2tog on the wrong side. Cut the yarn and pull it through the last stitch. To knit the square in stockinette stitch, work the decrease in 3 of every 4 rows.

In the introduction I mentioned a set of small wooden blocks I played with as a child. This intarsia technique allows me to replicate the designs I made then and brings the same feelings of play and exploration. The design possibilities can be explored with any computer paint program, on grid paper, or by making two colored paper cutouts that can be arranged and rearranged.

Of course, you are not limited to two colors when using this technique. For example, you could gather a group of compatible light-colored yarns and another group of darker yarns. After planning a design, randomly select from the light or dark yarns, according to your grid. Or, work with a monochromatic color scheme, shading from dark to light. Try knitting with three, four, or many colors, having one or two main colors and several accent colors.

DRAMATIC DIAGONALS

Another method of changing colors within a mitered square is to knit the square itself in one color, while working the decreases in a contrasting yarn (shown in the swatch here and in Stained Glass on page 68). The decrease technique in which a center slip-stitch line is formed by double decreases (S2KP2) is used here.

The basic square is knit as described on page 44, except that when it's time to knit the decrease, drop the main yarn and pick up the contrast yarn (which is hanging on the wrong side of the work). Complete the decrease with the contrast yarn, drop it, and finish the row with the main yarn. On wrong-side rows (without decreases), purl the center stitch and work the next stitch in the contrast yarn, then finish the row in the

Four intarsia mitered squares

Intarsia mitered squares

Explore the design possibilities

Decrease and first 2 rows worked in contrast color

Color contrast emphasizes the decrease line

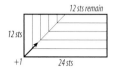

A mitered rectangle

Building with mitered rectangles

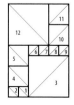

**Big and little squares–
all squares are a multiple of the
smallest square**

main yarn. The reason for this maneuver is so that on the following row, the two slipped stitches in the double decrease will both be in the contrast color yarn, which makes a neater center line.

In the swatch, the initial pick-up or cast-on row and the next (wrong-side) row were also worked in the contrast yarn, adding yet another dimension to the design. Here's a tip for working with a contrast yarn that's especially useful if you plan to make many squares: measure the length of contrast yarn needed for one square, then cut a piece of the contrast yarn before beginning each square. I find it easier to work with these shorter lengths for the contrasting center line.

Just as with the mitered intarsia technique, this addition of another color changes and increases the design possibilities.

MITERS DON'T HAVE TO BE SQUARE!
There is no reason that the decrease line has to be in the center of the row. As long as a decrease line is maintained, there can be any number of stitches before or after the decrease line.

Try a rectangle knit in this manner: cast on 24 stitches for one side of the rectangle, one stitch for the double-decrease line, and 12 stitches for the other side of the rectangle. The knitting proceeds as usual for a mitered square: knit until there are no more stitches on one side of the square. In this example, when stitches run out on one side, 12 stitches remain on the other side.

BUILDING WITH MITERED RECTANGLES
There are several options for these remaining 12 stitches. For example, they can be bound off, which results in a rectangle that is twice as wide as it is tall. These stitches could also be used as the beginning stitches of another rectangle or square.

BIG SQUARES, LITTLE SQUARES
If you've taken any design classes, you know that repetition and proportion are basic principles of good design. We're already employing repetition when we knit several of these mitered squares. Changing the size or proportion of the squares will add variety to your mitered square knitting. An occasional line of very small squares, many medium-sized squares, and a few very large squares can draw the eye in, adding interest and excitement to your design. Using grid paper or a computer paint program, you can experiment until you come up with some pleasing designs.

One of the easiest ways to work with different-sized squares is to decide on a base number of stitches for your smallest square and then use multiples of this number for the larger squares. I've sketched two designs using this technique. The numbers suggest the order in which the squares might be knit.

PARTIAL MITERED SQUARES
What would happen if you were to knit a mitered square, but half way through the process, you bound off all the stitches? You would have an L-shaped piece of knitting

miters ✚ beyond

with a miter line in the corner of the L. Once again, new possibilities arise. These L shapes could be stacked, rotated, or turned on their points and stacked to form a chevron-like pattern.

AN ENTIRE JACKET CAN BE CREATED OF JUST 4 LARGE L SHAPES:
1 I started this jacket by casting on the stitches for the center back (line A-B) using a temporary cast on so that I could later knit these same stitches in the opposite direction. I knit this section until I reached the edge of the back neck (about 3½").
2 Then I cast on enough stitches for the length of the shoulder and sleeve (line C-D). I knit this mitered section until I had enough fabric for half of the sleeve and half of the back (about 9½" more) and then I bound off all the stitches.
3, 4 I went back to the center back stitches and repeated the same process for the other half of the back and left sleeve.
5 Then I picked up the shoulder stitches along line C-D and cast on enough stitches for the jacket front (line C-E). I knit another partial mitered square, the same size as the back section.
6 Next, I repeated the process for the other half of the jacket front.
7, 8 Finally, I picked up stitches along line C-E, did some neck shaping, and finished the right front, then finished the left front. A shaping detail I added to the second of these jackets was short-row shaping to taper the sleeves, for a closer fit.

2-, 3-, AND 4-SQUARE MODULES
After I had been designing with basic mitered squares for a while, rotating them this way and that, I suddenly realized that I could cast on enough stitches for 2 squares at one time. A little more work and I saw that if I could knit 2 squares at one time, I could just as easily knit 3 or 4 squares at once.

Some time later, I became acquainted with the work of Horst Schulz and saw the many wonderful designs he has created using what he calls 2-in-1, 3-in-1, and 4-in-1 motifs. This development of mitered squares provides many design options, since single, double, triple, and quadruple squares can be combined in one design.

Let's look at the steps involved in planning and knitting a piece with 3-square modules. The first step is to decide on the size of a single square. In this example, the square is 12 stitches on each side. To accommodate the double decrease, cast on one stitch in each corner. So, this basic square will have a total of 12 + 12 + 1 = 25 stitches. Once this base number of stitches is calculated, multiply it (25) by the number of squares to be knit. For a 3-square module, cast on 3 × 25 = 75 stitches. I find that it's easiest to think of each square separately as I'm working, so on my first decrease row, I would say to myself, "Knit 11, work a double decrease, knit 11." This finishes the first of the 3 squares; placing a marker here can help. Then I would repeat the same numbers for the second and third squares.

After completing this module, I might pick up stitches wherever I want and knit a different motif. To me, this is play!

Partial mitered squares can be stacked...

rotated...

or form chevrons

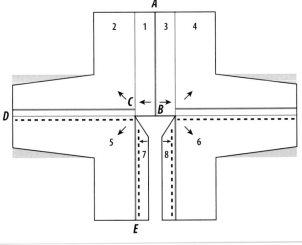

A jacket made of 4 L shapes

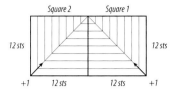

Square 2 | Square 1

12 sts | 12 sts

+1 | 12 sts | 12 sts | +1

2-square module

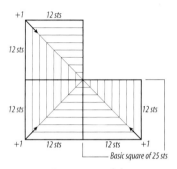

+1 | 12 sts

12 sts

12 sts | 12 sts

+1 | 12 sts | 12 sts | +1

Basic square of 25 sts

3-square module

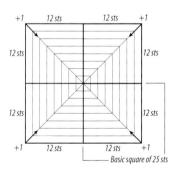

+1 | 12 sts | 12 sts | +1

12 sts | 12 sts

12 sts | 12 sts

+1 | 12 sts | 12 sts | +1

Basic square of 25 sts

4-square module

PATTERNS

Two vests, Mariposa, page 66, and Stained Glass, page 68, make use of contrast-color diagonals. Intarsia squares add drama to Mariposa. Except for the heels and toes, the Swatch Your Step Socks, page 70, are all 2-square modules. Mendocino, page 64, combines 1-, 2-, and 3-square modules.

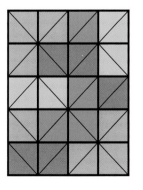

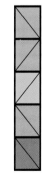

Playing with 1-, 2-, 3-, and 4-square modules

miters + beyond

WORK IT OUT

The grid on page 114 is perfect for placing squares and miters.

Mariposa, p. 66

Mendocino, p. 64

Right or wrong— either side works.

Stained Glass, p. 68

Work the decreases with a contrasting color.

GINGER LU

SWATCH TRICKS
Singles, doubles, and triples fit together like puzzle pieces.

Mohair for her, classic wool for him.

Mendocino

NOTES
1 See *Techniques*, page 116, for ssk, p2tog, S2KP2, wrap and turn (W&T), 3-needle bind-off. **2** In these instructions "pick up" means "pick up and knit." Pick up all stitches with RS facing. **3** Refer to Map for placement of Mitered Squares and Half-Squares and direction of work. **4** Sleeves are knit side to side, beginning and ending at top of arm.

GARTER RIDGE PATTERN
Rows 1, 3 (RS) Knit.
Row 2 Knit.
Row 4 Purl.
Repeat Rows 1–4 for Garter Ridge Pattern.

⚃ BASIC MITERED SQUARE
Row 1 (RS) With larger needles and A, cast on (or pick up, depending on where you are on the Map) 22 (24, 26) sts.
Row 2 Knit.
Row 3 Change to MC, k9 (10, 11), ssk, k2tog, k9 (10, 11).
Row 4 Purl.
Row 5 K8 (9, 10), ssk, k2tog, k8 (9, 10).
Row 6 Knit.
Continue to work in Garter Ridge Pattern and work 2 decreases in the center of each RS row until 2 sts remain.
Next row (WS) P2tog, fasten off. Basic Square measures approximately 3½ (3¾, 4)".

⚃ 2-SQUARE MODULE
Row 1 (RS) With larger needles and A, cast on or pick up 22 (24, 26) sts, place marker (pm), cast on or pick up 22 (24, 26) more sts.
Continue as 2 Basic Squares (working each row of instructions twice) until 4 sts remain.
Next row (WS) P4tog, fasten off.

⚃ 3-SQUARE MODULE
Row 1 (RS) With larger needles and A, cast on or pick up 22 (24, 26) sts, pm, cast on or pick up 22 (24, 26) more sts, pm, cast on or pick up 22 (24, 26) more sts.
Continue as 3 Basic Squares (working each row of instructions 3 times) until 6 sts remain.
Next row (WS) P6.

Next row S2KP2 twice. Slip first st over second, fasten off.

△ HALF-SQUARE MODULE
Row 1 With A, pick up 22 (24, 26) sts.
Row 2 Knit.
With MC, continue as Basic Square, AT SAME TIME, work ssk at the beginning and k2tog at the end of all RS rows until 8 sts remain.
Next row (RS) Ssk, ssk, k2tog, k2tog.
Bind off purlwise, slipping first st.

RIGHT FRONT, LEFT FRONT, AND BACK
Beginning with Square 1 and following the numbers on the Maps, work Basic Square, 2- Square, 3-Square, and Half-Square Modules. Block pieces lightly.

SHOULDER SHAPINGS
Note For Right Shoulder (shaded on Map), pick up sts on Right Front; for Left Shoulder, pick up sts on Back.
Row 1 (RS) With A, pick up 12 (13, 14) sts.
Rows 2–4 Knit.
Row 5 K10, wrap next st and turn (W&T).
WS Rows Knit to end.
Short Row 7 K7, W&T.
Row 9 Knit all sts.
Short Row 11 K7, W&T.
Short Row 13 K10, W&T.
Next 3 rows Knit all sts.
Bind off.
Sew Right Shoulder to Back; sew Left Shoulder to Left Front.

SLEEVES
Row 1 With larger needle and A, cast on 65 (68, 71) sts.
Row 2 Knit.
Short Rows 3, 4 K14, W&T, purl to end.
Short Rows 5, 6 K20, W&T, knit to end.
With MC, continue in Garter Ridge Pattern, AT SAME TIME, on each RS row work 6 more sts before W&T until 62 sts are knit.
Next 2 rows With A, knit all sts.
With MC, continue in Garter Ridge Pattern for 22 (22, 26) more rows.

This fun-to-knit jacket is composed of 1-, 2-, and 3-square modules that are knit in a lovely hand-dyed yarn. Each section is outlined in a solid color, which sets it off and emphasizes the unique shapes.

Next row With A, bind off 13 (14, 15) sts, knit remaining sts.

Next row Knit to bound-off section, cast on 13 (14, 15) sts.

With MC, continue in Garter Ridge Pattern for 22 (22, 26) more rows.

Next 2 rows With A, knit.

Next row With MC, k62, W&T, purl to end.

Next row K56, W&T, knit to end.

Continue in Garter Ridge Pattern, AT SAME TIME, on each RS row work 6 sts fewer before W&T until 14 sts are knit.

Next 2 rows Knit all sts.

Bind off.

Block sleeve to desired dimensions.

CUFF

Row 1 With smaller needle and A, pick up 26 (26, 30) sts along bottom of Sleeve.

Row 2 Knit.

Rows 3, 4 With B, knit.

Rows 5–8 With A, knit.

Bind off.

Bottom bands

With smaller needles and A, pick up 33 (36, 39) sts along bottom Left Front and work as Cuff. Bind off. Repeat for Right Front.

For Back, pick up 66 (72, 78) sts and work as Cuff.

FINISHING

Sew seam along top of Sleeve.

With larger needle and A, pick up 61 (61, 65) sts along top of Sleeve. With separate needle, pick up 61 (62, 65) sts along straight edge of armhole. Attach Sleeve to Jacket, using 3-needle bind-off. Work side seams in same way, using 3-needle bind-off to join 49 (53, 57) sts picked up along sides of Fronts and Back.

FRONT AND NECK BAND

Row 1 With smaller needle and A, beginning at lower Right Front corner, pick up 53 (60, 64) sts to Half-Square 8, pm, pick up 15 (16, 17) sts to shoulder shaping, 36 sts along Back neck to front edge of Left Shoulder shaping, 15 (16, 17) sts along Half-Square 8, pm, 53 (60, 64) sts along Left Front edge—186 (198, 210) sts.

FIESTA YARNS La Boheme 4 (4, 5) skeins Sandstone (MC); Kokopelli 3 skeins color K22 Buckaroo Blue (A) and 1 skein K07 Cajeta (B); shown in Medium

Basic Square Size

	S	M	L
Inches	3½	3¾	4
Stitches	9+4+9	10+4+10	11+4+11

——— Cast on
- - - - Pick up and knit
——→ Direction of knitting

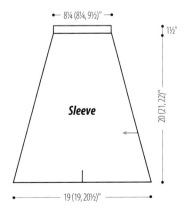

Sleeve

8¼ (8¼, 9½)"

1½"

20 (21, 22)"

19 (19, 20½)"

Row 2 (WS) Knit, increasing 1 (knit into front and back of st) in st after first marker and st before second marker, AT SAME TIME, work k2tog at each side where shoulder shaping meets Jacket Back.

Row 3 Knit.

Row 4 Repeat Row 2.

Row 5 Make buttonholes: K3, * yarn over, k2tog, k9 (10, 11); repeat from * for a total of six buttonholes, knit to end.

Row 6 Repeat Row 2.

Rows 7, 8 With B, repeat Rows 3, 4.

Rows 9, 10 With A, repeat Rows 3, 4.

Bind off loosely.

Sew underarm seam. Sew on buttons to match buttonholes. Sew in ends and block lightly.

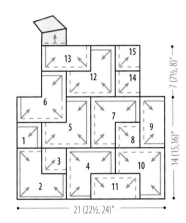

21 (22½, 24)"

7 (7½, 8)"

14 (15, 16)"

Back Map

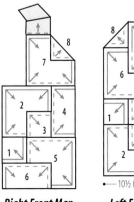

10½ (11¼, 12)"

Right Front Map   **Left Front Map**

Mariposa

Intermediate

LOOSE FIT

S (M, L)

Measures approximately
A 40 (43, 46)"
B 20 (21¼, 22½)"

10cm/4"

28   GET GAUGE!
19

over Garter Ridge Pattern

1 2 3 **4** 5 6

Medium weight

A 60 (65, 70) yds
B 200 (230, 250) yds
C 260 (290, 325) yds
D 150 (165, 180)yd
E 180 (200, 220)yds

4.5mm/US 7
or size to obtain gauge

4.5mm/US 7
74cm (29") long
for Bottom and Front Bands

Four 22mm/¾" buttons

Stitch markers

NOTES

1 See *Techniques*, page 116, for ssk and S2KP2.
2 Slip the last st of each row purlwise with yarn in front. On next row, knit into the back of the first stitch. *3* When changing colors, bring new color under old color to prevent holes. *4* In these instructions, "pick up" means "pick up and knit." Pick up all stitches with RS facing. *5* Refer to Map for placement and color of Mitered Squares, direction of knitting, and edges to be sewn.

GARTER RIDGE PATTERN

Rows 1, 3 (RS) Knit.
Row 2 (WS) Knit.
Row 4 Purl.
Repeat Rows 1–4 for Garter Ridge Pattern.

BASIC MITERED SQUARE

Before beginning, cut a strand of A 45 (49, 53)" long.
Row 1 Cast on (or pick up, depending on where you are on the Map), 14 (16, 18) sts in first color for the square, 1 st with color A, 14 (16, 18) sts with second color for that square.
Row 2 (WS) K14 (16, 18) sts with second color, p2 with A, k13 (15, 17) with first color.
Row 3 Knit to 1 st before center st with first color, work S2KP2 with A, knit remaining sts with second color—2 sts decreased.
Row 4 Purl to center st with second color, p2 with A, purl remaining sts with first color.
Row 5 Repeat Row 3.
Row 6 Knit to center st with second color, p2 with A, knit to end with first color.
Repeat Rows 3–6 until 3 sts remain and a WS row has been worked. Work S2KP2 with A. Fasten off. Basic Square measures approximately 3¼ (3½, 3¾)" when joined to other squares.

BACK

Beginning with Square 1 and following the numbers on the Map, work Basic Squares.

RIGHT FRONT

Following the Map, work Squares 27–38.
Half-Square 39
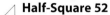
With B, pick up 14 (16, 18) sts along Square 32,

beginning at lower edge. Work in Garter Ridge Pattern, AT SAME TIME, k2tog at end of every RS row 13 (15, 17) times. Fasten off.

LEFT FRONT

Following the Map, work Squares 40–51.
Half-Square 52
Row 1 With E, pick up 14 (16, 18) sts along Square 45; with A, pick up 1 st in corner of Square 46; with C, pick up 14 (16, 18) sts along Square 40.
Row 2 and all following rows Work a Basic Square, AT SAME TIME, work ssk at the beginning and k2tog at the end of every RS row. When 5 sts remain and a WS row has been worked, with A, slip 2, k3tog, psso. Fasten off.

FINISHING

Sew edges of squares together where necessary. Sew shoulder seams.
Armhole edging
Row 1 With A, pick up 1 st in each garter ridge and 1 st in each St st section around armhole opening.
Row 2 Knit.
Row 3 With C, knit, working S2KP2 in each underarm corner.
Row 4 Knit.
Row 5 With A, knit, working S2KP2 in each underarm corner.
Bind off.
Sew side seams.
Bottom band
Row 1 (RS) With circular needle and A, pick up 1 st in each garter ridge and 1 st in each st section along entire bottom of vest. Count sts and increase (or decrease) if necessary on next row to get a multiple of 4 + 2.
Row 2 Knit.
Row 3 * With A, k2; with D, p2; repeat from *, end k2 with A.
Row 4 * With A, p2; with D, k2; repeat from *, end p2 with A.
Rows 5, 6 Repeat Rows 3, 4.
Rows 7, 8 Work Rows 3, 4 with A and B.
Rows 9, 10 Work Rows 3, 4 with A and C.
Rows 11, 12 Work Rows 3, 4 with A and E.
Rows 13, 14 With A, knit.
Bind off.

Each mitered square is knit in two colors with a black diagonal line dividing the two.
The colors are placed to form a large intarsia-like diamond pattern.

Front Band

Mark for four buttonholes, with the lower one 1" up from the bottom of the band and the top one 1" down from the top of Square 27 (or Square 40 for men's) and the other two spaced evenly between.

Row 1 With A, pick up along right center Front, neck, and left center Front. Mark the sts that are at the top and bottom of Squares 39 and 52 on the Vest Fronts.

Row 2 Knit.

Rows 3, 4 With D, knit.

Row 5 With A, knit, making buttonholes by binding off 2 sts at each buttonhole marker, increasing 1 st each side of marker at bottom of Squares 39 and 52, working an S2KP2 decrease at top of marked squares (slipping the st before the marked st and the marked st) and working 4 evenly spaced decreases (k2tog) across back neck section.

Row 6 Knit, casting on 2 sts over bound-off sts.

Rows 7, 8 With C, knit.

Row 9 Repeat Row 5, EXCEPT omit buttonholes.

Row 10 Knit.

Bind off.

Sew on buttons, sew in ends, and block lightly.

BRYSPUN Kid-n-Ewe 1 ball black 110 (A); 2 (2, 3) balls lavender 290 (B); 3 balls rust 510 (C); 2 balls each turquoise 490 (D) and light green 260 (E); shown in Small

---

Cast on
Pick up and knit
Seam
Direction of knitting

Color Key
■ A
□ B
□ C
□ D
□ E

Module Size

	S	M	L
Inches	3¼	3½	3¾
Stitches	14+1+14	16+1+16	18+1+18

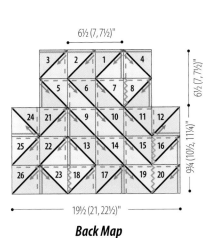

Back Map

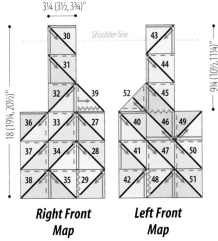

Right Front Map

Left Front Map

Stained Glass

NOTES

1 See *Techniques*, page 116, for p2tog, Make 1 (M1), ssk, ssp, SSSK, S2PP2, and S2KP2. *2* In these instructions, "pick up" means "pick up and knit." Pick up all stitches with RS facing. *3* Refer to the Map for placement of Mitered Squares, direction of work, and edges to be sewn. *4* Vest is worked in two separate panels, which are then sewn together at center back. *5* Twist yarns on WS at color change to prevent holes.

GARTER RIDGE PATTERN

Rows 1, 3 (RS) Knit.
Row 2 Knit.
Row 4 Purl.
Repeat Rows 1–4 for pattern.

BASIC SQUARE

Row 1 With CC, cast on (or pick up and knit, depending on where you are on the Map) 29 (31, 33) sts.
Row 2 (WS) Knit. Cut CC. Cut a new strand of CC 40 (43, 46)" long.
Row 3 With MC, k13 (14, 15); with CC strand, S2KP2; with MC, knit to end.
Row 4 Purl to CC st; with CC, p2; with MC, purl to end.
Rows 5, 7 Knit to CC sts; with CC, S2KP2; with MC, knit to end.
Row 6 Knit to CC st; with CC, p2; with MC, knit to end.
Rows 8–27 (8–29, 8–31) Repeat Rows 4–7, ending with Row 5 (7, 5).
Next row (WS) With CC, S2PP2. Fasten off. Basic Mitered Square measures 3¼ (3½, 3¾)" when joined to other squares.

LEFT PANEL

Beginning with Square 1 and following the Map, work shaded Triangle as follows:

Triangle 13

Row 1 With CC, pick up 28 (30, 32) sts along Squares 8 and 7, 1 st in corner, and 14 (15, 16) sts along edge of Square 10—43 (46, 49) sts.
Row 2 (WS) Knit. Cut CC. Cut a new CC strand approximately 30" long.

Row 3 With MC, bind off 1 st, ssk, k23 (25, 27); with CC, S2KP2; with MC, k10 (11, 12), k2tog, k1.
Row 4 Purl to CC st; with CC, p2; with MC, purl to last 3 sts, ssp, p1.
Rows 5, 7 Bind off 1 st, ssk, knit to CC sts; with CC, S2KP2; with MC, knit to last 3 sts, k2tog, k1.
Row 6 Knit to CC st; with CC, p2; with MC, knit to last 3 sts, ssk, k1.
Rows 8–11 (8–11, 8–15) [Repeat Rows 4–7] 1 (1, 2) times.
Rows 12–14 (12–14, 16) [Repeat Row(s) 4–6 (4–6, 4)] once more—7 (10, 7) sts.
Sizes S (L) only: Row 15 (17) (RS) With MC, SSSK; with CC, S2KP2; with MC, k1.
Row 16 (18) With CC, S2PP2. Fasten off.
Size M only: Row 15 (RS) Bind off 1 st, ssk, k1; with CC, S2KP2; with MC, k2.
Row 16 With MC, p2; with CC, p1; with MC, ssp, p1.
Row 17 With MC, k1; with CC, S2KP2; with MC, k1.
Row 18 With CC, S2PP2. Fasten off.

RIGHT PANEL

Triangle 13

Row 1 With CC, pick up and k14 (15, 16) sts along Square 10, 1 st in corner, and 28 (30, 32) sts along Squares 7 and 8—43 (46, 49) sts.
Row 2 (WS) Knit. Cut CC and cut new strand of CC as before.
Row 3 With MC, k1, ssk, k10 (11, 12); with CC strand, S2KP2; with MC, knit to last 3 sts, k2tog, k1.
Row 4 Bind off 1 st, p2tog, purl to CC st; with CC, p2; with MC, purl to end.
Rows 5, 7 K1, ssk, knit to CC sts; with CC, S2KP2; with MC, knit to last 3 sts, k2tog, k1.
Row 6 Bind off 1 st, k2tog, knit to CC st; with CC, p2; with MC, knit to end.
Continue to work as Triangle 13, Left Panel, EXCEPT reverse shaping.

FINISHING

Sew panels together at center back. Block piece.
Armhole edging
With circular needle and CC, pick up 98 (105, 112) sts around armhole edge. Bind off knitwise, working k2tog at each underarm corner.
Sew shoulder seams.

In this striking vest, a secondary pattern is created by working the diagonal decreases in a contrasting color yarn.

Right front lower edge band

Note Sl sts purlwise with yarn at WS.

With CC, pick up 43 (45, 49) sts along lower edge of right front (Squares 1, 6, and 12).

Row 1 (WS) Knit.

Row 2,3 With MC, * k1, sl 1; repeat from *, end k1.

Rows 4, 5 With CC, knit.

Rows 6–13 [Repeat Rows 2–5] twice.

Row 14 With CC, knit. Bind off knitwise.

Left front lower edge band

Work as for right front band, picking up sts along Squares 12, 6, and 1.

Back lower edge band

Work as for front bands, picking up 85 (91, 97) sts along lower edge of back.

Side vent edgings

With CC, pick up 19 (20, 21) sts along each side of vent—38 (40, 42) sts. Bind off knitwise, working k2tog at top of vent.

Front and neck band

With circular needle and CC, pick up 5 sts along lower right front band, 13 (14, 15) sts along each of next 3 squares, 1 st at top corner of last square, place marker (pm), 21 (23, 25) sts along triangle, 13 (14, 15) sts along next square, 27 (29, 31) sts along back neck, 13 (14, 15) sts along next square of left front, 21 (23, 25) sts along triangle, then 1 st at top corner of next square, pm, 13 (14, 15) sts along each of next 3 squares, 5 sts along lower band—185 (199, 213) sts.

Row 1 (WS) Knit, M1 at each marked point, and working k2tog at each back neck corner and at center of each back neck square—183 (197, 211) sts.

Row 2 (buttonhole row) With MC, [k1, sl 1] 2 (3, 2) times, * bind off 2 sts, [sl 1, k1] 4 (4, 5) times, sl 1; repeat from * twice more, bind off 2 sts, * sl 1, k1; repeat from * to end.

Row 3 K1, sl 1; repeat from *, casting on 2 sts over each pair of bound-off sts, end k1.

Rows 4, 5 With CC, knit.

Bind off knitwise. Sew on buttons.

MOUNTAIN COLORS Mountain Goat 3 skeins Crazy Woman (MC); 1 (1, 2) skeins Deep Blue (CC); shown in Medium.

Module Size

	S	M	L
Inches	3¼	3½	3¾
Stitches	14+1+14	15+1+15	16+1+16

——— Cast on
- - - - Pick up and knit
wwww Seam
——→ Direction of knitting

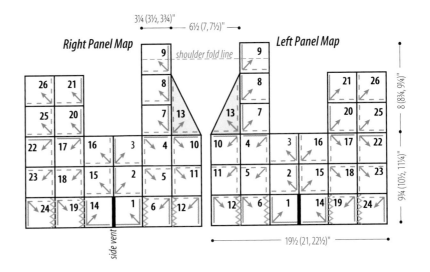

Swatch Your Step

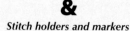
NOTES

1 See *Techniques*, page 116, for ssk, S2KP2, grafting, cable cast-on, and 3-needle bind-off. *2* In these instructions, "pick up" means "pick up and knit". Pick up stitches with RS facing. *3* Use straight needles for leg and instep portions of sock. Double-pointed needles are required for toe shaping and for 3-needle bind-off. *4* Slip sts purlwise with yarn at WS of work.

GARTER RIDGE PATTERN

Rows 1, 3 (RS) Knit.
Row 2 Knit.
Row 4 Purl.
Repeat Rows 1–4 for Garter Ridge Pattern.

BASIC MITERED SQUARE

Row 1 With A, cast on 13 sts, pick up (or knit, depending on where you are on the Map) 12 sts—25 sts.
Row 2 (WS) Knit.
Row 3 With B, k11, S2KP2, k11.
Row 4 Purl.
Row 5 With A, k10, S2KP2, k10.
Row 6 K10, p1, k10. Continue to work in Garter Ridge Pattern and work 2 decreases at miter on RS rows until 1 st remains.
Fasten off.

2-Square Module

1 Half-Leg Section

12 sts

12 sts

12 sts   center marker   12 sts

corner st   corner st

3

2

1

2-SQUARE MODULE

Row 1 With A, cast on 13 sts, pick up (or knit, depending on where you are on the Map) 12 sts, place marker (pm), pick up or knit 12 more sts; cable cast on 13 sts—50 sts until 2 sts remain. Continue as 2 Basic Squares (working each row of instructions twice) until 2 sts remain.
Next row (WS) P2tog. Fasten off.

1 HALF-LEG SECTION (make 2)

With A, cast on 24 sts loosely.
Begin Rib Pattern
Row 1 (RS) K1, * p2, k2; repeat from *, end p2, k1.
Row 2 P1, * k2, p2; repeat from *, end k2, p1.
Rows 3–10 Repeat Rows 1 and 2. Break yarn.

Module 1

Work 2-Square Module—knitting center 24 sts into rib sts.

Modules 2 and 3

Work as Module 1, except pick up center 24 sts along top edge of preceding module.

2 JOIN SECTIONS

With dpn and A, begin at top of ribbing of first Half-Leg Section and pick up 7 sts along ribbing and 12 sts along each module edge—43 sts. With 2nd needle, pick up 43 sts along other Half-Leg Section, beginning with third module. Join seam, using 3-needle bind-off (ridge to RS).

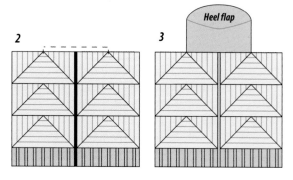

2   3   Heel flap

3 Heel Flap

With A, pick up 26 sts from center point of one module to center point of other. Turn and purl 26. Continue working 26 sts of heel flap as follows:
Row 1 (RS) * Sl 1, k1; repeat from *.
Row 2 Sl 1, p25.
Repeat these 2 rows 11 times more (for a total of 12 chain sts along each edge).

Turn heel

Row 1 (RS) Sl 1, k13, ssk, k1, turn.
Row 2 Sl 1, p3, p2tog, p1, turn.
Row 3 Sl 1, k4, ssk, k1, turn.
Row 4 Sl 1, p5, p2tog, p1, turn.

Here's a toasty pair of socks designed in true modular form: with one set of numbers in the pattern, simply increase the needle size for the larger sock size. What could be easier?

Row 5 Sl 1, k6, ssk, k1, turn.
Row 6 Sl 1, p7, p2tog, p1, turn.
Row 7 Sl 1, k8, ssk, k1, turn.
Row 8 Sl 1, p9, p2tog, p1, turn.
Row 9 Sl 1, k10, ssk, k1, turn.
Row 10 Sl 1, p11, p2tog, p1, turn.
Row 11 Sl 1, k12, ssk.
Row 12 Sl 1, p12, p2tog—14 sts. Break yarn.

4 HEEL GUSSET / INSTEP

Row 1 (RS) With 2nd needle and A, cast on 13 sts, pick up 12 sts along module, pm, pick up 12 sts along edge of heel flap, k14 heel sts, pick up 12 sts along other edge of heel flap, pm, pick up 12 sts along module, cast on 13 sts—88 sts. (The first and last 25 sts on your needle form the instep, and each side is worked like a Basic Mitered Square. The center 38 sts form the gussets and sole.)
Row 2 Knit.
Row 3 With B, * k11, S2KP2, k11 *, ssk, knit to 2 sts before marker, k2tog; repeat from * to *.
Row 4 Purl.
Row 5 With A, * k10, S2KP2, k10 *, ssk, knit to 2 sts before marker, k2tog; repeat from * to *. Continue in patterns as established, working Basic Mitered Square at each side for instep, and decrease 1 st at each side of gusset sts between markers until there are 24 sts between markers (7 gusset decs have been worked on each side of heel). Don't work any more gusset decreases (but continue working Garter Ridge Pattern over these sts), and continue working pattern as established over instep sts until there are 3 instep sts at each side and 24 gusset sts between markers.
Next row (WS) With B, p3tog, remove marker, p2tog, p20, p2tog, remove marker, p3tog—24 sts.

5 INSTEP

** With 2nd needle and A, cable cast on 13 sts, pick up 12 sts along edge of Mitered Square just completed, pm, k24 sts from needle, pm, pick up 12 sts along 2nd Mitered Square, cable cast on 13 sts—74 sts. Work Mitered Square over first and last 25 sts and work Garter Ridge Pattern even over center 24 sts until 30 sts remain.

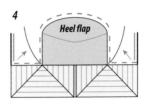

4

Heel flap

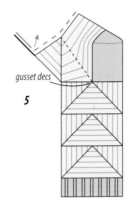

gusset decs

5

——— Join with 3-needle bind-off
———— Cast on
- - - - Pick up and knit
- - - - Knit live stitches
→ Direction of knitting

Next row (WS) With B, p3tog, p2tog, p20, p2tog, p3tog—24 sts. ** Repeat from ** to ** once more. Place sts on hold and lightly block.

Join center front seam

With A, join seam as for back seam, using 3-needle bind-off, picking up 12 sts at each mitered section and 7 sts in each ribbing—79 sts.

SHAPE TOE

24 sts remaining from instep are bottom of toe. With A, pick up 24 sts across top of toe section—48 sts. Divide sts onto 4 dpns—12 on each dpn. (At this point, if any extra length is needed in the foot section, knit several rnds even with yarn A.)
Begin decreases
Rnd 1 * K1, ssk, knit to end of needle; on 2nd needle, knit to last 3 sts, k2tog, k1; repeat from * once more for top of toe section.
Rnd 2 Knit. Repeat Rnds 1 and 2 until there are 9 sts on each needle, then repeat Rnd 1 until there are 4 sts on each needle. Cut yarn, leaving a long tail and graft top and bottom sections together.

Lorna's Laces Shepherd Sock Yarn, 1 skein each 37NS Violet (A) and 18 Watercolor (B); shown in Small/Medium

stunning strips

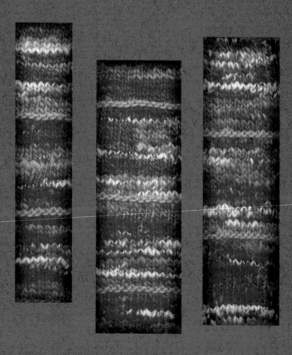

stunning strips

Knitting strips is another of my favorite techniques. The knitting is done on a small number of stitches, so the work is portable and grows quickly. Design and color options are greatly expanded when the strips are combined. In a finished strip garment, there may appear to be many color changes in one row, although only one or two colors may have been used in any row of a single strip.

THE BASICS: PLANNING A SIMPLE STRIP VEST

The easiest way to plan a strip project is to begin with a schematic of the garment. The simpler the shaping, the easier it will be to plan. Then, make some basic decisions about the strips. Will they be narrow or wide? Will they all be the same width? Will the entire garment be composed of strips?

Let's step through the process of working a simple vest in strips. Begin by selecting a vest pattern and drawing its outline on graph paper or the grid on page 114, with each square representing one inch. To experiment with various strip widths and placements, make several copies of this outline, or use a computer program, as I do.

Since each grid square equals one inch, the size of each strip can be quickly determined by counting the squares on the schematic. For a 42" vest with 6 equal-width strips across the front, each strip will be 3½" wide. The next step is to knit a swatch and measure the stitch gauge. Then cast on the required number of stitches for the strip and start knitting.

SIMPLE STRIPS

The knitting can be simple or complex. No matter which approach you choose, your garment will have visual interest and complexity that is not obvious from the individual strips. Some of the easiest strip techniques such as knitting with hand-dyed yarns or creating random stripes can produce rich garments.

The stripes and splotches that often appear when hand-dyed or variegated yarns are knit across the width of a garment will not be a problem when knitting strips, and any that do appear contribute to the overall effect. Multicolored yarns can also be combined with one or more solid colors to accentuate the variegation.

Stripes, either random or carefully planned, can yield exciting results with little effort. When strips are placed next to each other, the juxtaposed stripes create interest. Blocks of color are also effective; their placement can be random or planned to create a pattern as a particular color or stitch pattern is repeated from one strip to another. The stripes could be knit in stockinette stitch, or reverse stockinette for an interesting, blended look, or in stitch patterns.

MORE COMPLEX STRIPS

There is no limit to what can be knit in strips. Combine small Fair Isle blocks with solid areas or other stitch patterns. Knit cables and other textured stitch patterns in strips of one or more colors. Try mosaic patterns for drama and color interaction (see De Colores, pages 81–83). Once you begin to experiment, more and more ideas will pop into your mind and off your needles.

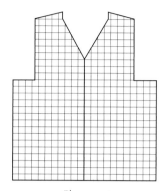

Plan a vest

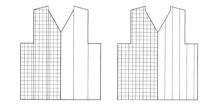

Experiment with strip widths

Interest grows when strips are joined

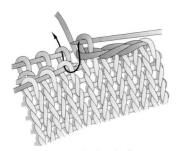

*3-needle bind-off
with ridge to right side*

Strips can taper...

angle in and out...

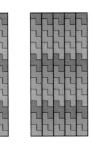

*and be made
of modules.*

JOINING STRIPS

After all the strips are knitted, the next step is to put them together. In practice, the joining technique should be considered prior to knitting the strips. Some of the many possible approaches require advance planning; others can be a last-minute decision. The most obvious method is to sew the strips together, using mattress stitch, just as for the side seams of any knitted garment. Sewing is not a bad choice, it's just less interesting and is the method I'm least likely to use. If I do sew the strips together, I might put the seams on the right side. Of course, I'd want my selvedge stitches to be perfect!

3-NEEDLE BIND-OFF

My favorite method of joining strips is the 3-needle bind-off, a technique often used to join the shoulders of a sweater. I like to work its small, neat ridge on the right side, as a design element. For further emphasis, I work this bind-off in a contrasting color, often black or navy.

If the strips are fairly long, mark each at the half and quarter points. I know what my stitch gauge is, so I know how many stitches should be picked up in each section. Pick up stitches along one edge of a strip. Cut the yarn and set the strip aside. Then pick up the same number of stitches along the matching edge of the other strip. Holding these two needles together in your left hand, use a third needle to work the bind-off (detailed on page 116). After a couple of inches, check that the bind-off is not too tight.

JOIN AS YOU GO

One way to join strips in a less visible manner is to knit them together as you go along. Begin by knitting the first strip on the far left of the garment piece. As you knit the second strip, join it to the first strip at the far end of every right-side row. A slip-stitch edge (see page 5) works best for this method. Since this method creates one slipped stitch for every two rows of knitting, simply work the join into each slipped edge stitch. For details, see page 7.

There are many other ways to join strips, including crochet or decorative embroidery stitches; experiment and choose what works best for your project.

ADVANCED TECHNIQUES

Strips need not be restricted to their simplest form. Shaping (short rows, increasing and decreasing) can be used to taper the strips from wide to narrow, creating an A-line or swing-line garment. Strips can also be composed of other module shapes, such as triangles.

PATTERNS

With a join-as-you-go pattern that spans sizes from a child's 2 to an adult's 1X, Morgan's Pullover, page 78, shows the range of sizing easily achieved with strips. The De Colores jacket, pages 81–83, is worked in a mosaic pattern and joined later with a 3-needle bind-off.

strips

WORK IT OUT

Use the grid on page 114 to arrange strips of colors and pattern.

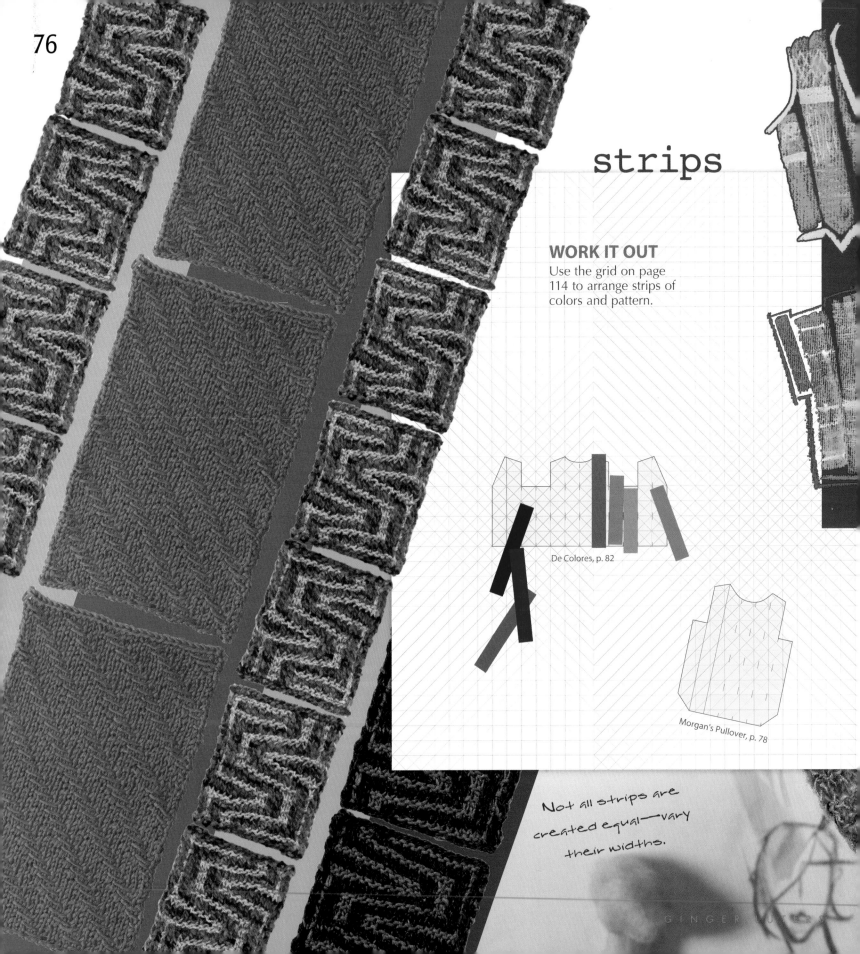

De Colores, p. 82

Morgan's Pullover, p. 78

Not all strips are created equal—vary their widths.

SWATCH TRICKS
Vertical strips can be worked separately or joined as you go.

The simplicity of strips allows for needle play and stitchwork.

MODULE MAGIC

Morgan's Pullover

Intermediate

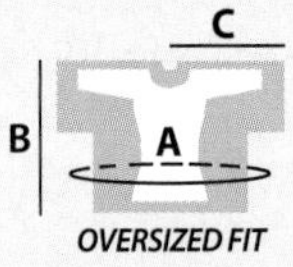

OVERSIZED FIT

Child 2 (4, 6, 8)
A 28 (30½, 31½, 35)"
B 12 (12¾, 14¼, 16)"
C 10¼ (10½, 11, 11½)"

Adult S [M, L, 1X]
A 41 [44, 47½, 51]"
B 22 [23, 24, 25]"
C 21¼ [21¼, 21¼, 21¼]"

10cm/4"

(48)
[30] GET GAUGE!
(28) [16]
over Garter Ridge pattern,
using larger needles

1 **2** 3 4 5 6

**Fine weight
Child**

MC 400 (455, 520, 625) yds
CC 200 (225, 255, 310) yds

1 2 3 **4** 5 6

**Medium weight
Adult**

MC 615 [687, 775, 865] yds
CC 410 [458, 515, 580] yds

(2.75 and 3.25mm/US 2 and 3)
[4 and 4.5mm/US 6 and 7]
or size to obtain gauge

4mm/G

&

Stitch holder

NOTES

1 See *Techniques*, page 116, for wrap and turn (W&T) for short rows, p2tog, cable cast-on, 3-needle bind-off, single crochet, and backwards single crochet. **2** In these instructions, "pick up" means "pick up and knit." Pick up all stitches with RS facing. **3** On all strips, work last st of each WS row by slipping last st purlwise, with yarn in front (wyif). **4** Begin each RS row by knitting the first stitch through the back loop (tbl). **5** Child sizes are given in parentheses; adult sizes follow in brackets. If there is only one figure or set of instructions, it applies to all sizes.

GARTER RIDGE PATTERN

Rows 1, 3 (RS) Knit.
Row 2 Knit.
Row 4 Purl.
Repeat Rows 1–4 for pattern.

BACK (Strips 1–7)

Strip 1
Note On this strip only, slip the last st on every row. With MC and larger needle, cast on 3 sts.
Knit 1 row (WS).
Work in Garter Ridge Pattern, beginning with Row 3 and increasing 1 st at end of every RS row until there are 11 (12, 13, 14) sts. Continue in Garter Ridge Pattern until (5¾, 6¼, 7, 7¾) [13¼, 13¾, 14¼, 14¾]" have been worked from beginning.
Bind off.
With CC, pick up (41, 43, 49, 55) [53, 55, 57, 59] sts along right edge of Strip 1 (pick up 1 st in each chain st along this edge). Cast on (25, 27, 31, 35) [35, 37, 39, 41] sts using cable cast-on—(66, 70, 80, 90) [88, 92, 96, 100] sts. Knit 2 rows, purl 1 row, knit 2 rows. Leave sts on needle.

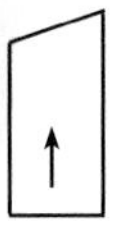

Strip 2
With MC, cast on 11 (12, 13, 14) sts onto empty needle, place last st onto needle holding CC sts and p2tog (one st of MC and one st of CC).
Turn work, slip first st knitwise, then knit this row (WS), remembering to work slipped edge st at the end of each WS row.
Continue working in Garter Ridge pattern, joining the strip you are knitting to the CC sts at the left edge of every RS row by p2tog and working the first

st of each WS row by slipping knitwise until 1 CC st remains.
Begin shoulder shaping: Next row (RS) K8, wrap and turn (W&T), work back in pattern.
Next row (RS) K4, W&T, work back in pattern.
Next row (RS) Knit across all sts, hiding short row wraps as you go. Bind off.
With CC, pick up stitches along edge of Strip 2, picking up 1 st in each slipped edge st—(69, 73, 83, 93) [91, 95, 99, 103] sts.
Knit 2 rows, purl 1 row, knit 1 row.
Next row (WS) Bind off (4) [11] sts, knit remaining sts—(65, 69, 79, 89) [80, 84, 88, 92] sts.

Strip 3
With MC, cast on 11 (12, 13, 14) sts and work as Strip 2, joining Strip sts to CC stitches for (9¼, 9¾, 11¼, 12¾) [20, 21, 22, 23]".
Begin neck shaping: Next row (RS) Bind off 5 (6, 7, 8) sts. Work across remaining sts.
Next 3 RS rows Bind off 2 sts. Work across remaining sts. Fasten off.
With CC, pick up (61, 65, 75, 85) [76, 80, 84, 88] sts along edge of Strip 3.
Knit 2 rows, purl 1 row, knit 2 rows.

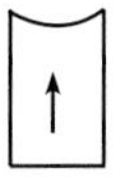

Strip 4
Work as Strip 2 until (8¾, 9¼, 10¾, 12¼)" [19, 20, 21, 22]" have been worked and all CC sts joined. Bind off.
With CC, pick up (61, 65, 75, 85) [76, 80, 84, 88] sts along edge of Strip 4.
Knit 2 rows, purl 1 row, knit 2 rows.

Strip 5
With MC, cast on 11 (12, 13, 14) sts and work as Strip 3, joining Strip sts to CC sts, for (8¾, 9¼, 10¾, 12¼) [19, 20, 21, 22]".
Begin neck shaping: Next row and all RS rows Work across.
Next row (WS) Bind off 5 (6, 7, 8) sts. Work across remaining sts.
Next 3 WS rows Bind off 2 sts. Work across remaining sts. Fasten off.
With CC, pick up (65, 69, 79, 89) [80, 84, 88, 92] sts along edge of Strip 5 and cast on (4) [11] sts—(69, 73, 83, 93) [91, 95, 99, 103] sts.
Knit 2 rows, purl 1 row, knit 2 rows.

Fourteen strips are joined together as you work, creating flattering vertical panels.
This fun-to-knit pullover can be knit in a variety of yarns to achieve several very different effects. Hand-dyed and variegated yarns work well in the strips, which are outlined with a contrasting solid-color yarn.

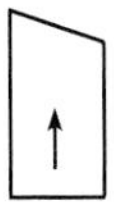

Strip 6

Work as Strip 2 up to shoulder shaping.
Shoulder shaping: Next row (WS) K4, W&T, knit back.
Next row (WS) K8, W&T, knit back.
Next row (WS) Knit across all sts, hiding short row wraps as you go.
Bind off all sts.
With CC, pick up (66, 70, 80, 90) [88, 92, 96, 100] sts along edge of Strip 6.
Knit 2 rows, purl 1 row, knit 1 row.
Next row (WS) Bind off (25, 27, 31, 35) [35, 37, 39, 41] sts and knit the remaining sts. Leave sts on needle—(41, 43, 49, 55) [53, 55, 57, 59] sts.

Strip 7

With MC, cast on 3 sts.
Knit 1 row (WS).
Work Garter Ridge pattern, increasing 1 st at beginning of every RS row until there are 11 (12, 13, 14) sts, AT SAME TIME, joining to the CC sts at the end of every RS row. Continue until (5¾, 6¼, 7, 7¾) [13¼, 13¾, 14¼, 14¾]" have been worked from beginning. Bind off.
With CC, pick up (33, 34, 39, 44) [45, 46, 47, 48] sts along edge of Strip 7.
Knit 2 rows, purl 1 row, knit 2 rows.

SWEATER FRONT (Strips 8–14)

Strip 8

Work as Strip 1, EXCEPT when 11 (12, 13, 14) MC sts on needle, join to CC sts attached to Strip 7.

Strip 9

Work as Strip 2, until it is time to bind off CC sts.
Bind off (8) [15] sts—(61, 65, 75, 85) [76, 80, 84, 88] sts.

Strip 10

Work as Strip 3 for (8¾, 9, 10¾, 12¼) [19, 20, 21, 22]".
At beginning of next RS row, bind off (2, 3, 4, 5) sts, then bind off 3 sts beginning of next 3 RS rows, fasten off.
With CC, pick up (57, 61, 71, 81) [72, 76, 80, 84] sts along edge.
Knit 2 rows, purl 1 row, knit 2 rows.

Strip 11

Work (8¼, 8¾, 10¼, 11½) [20¼]" in pattern.
Bind off.

With CC, pick up (57, 61, 71, 81) [72, 76, 80, 84] sts along edge.
Knit 2 rows, purl 1 row, knit 2 rows.

Strip 12

Work as Strip 3 for (8¼, 8¾, 10¼, 11½) [19¼, 20¼, 21¼, 22½]".
At beginning of next WS row, bind off 2 (3, 4, 5) sts then bind off 3 sts at beginning of next 3 WS rows, fasten off.

Module Size Child

	2	4	6	8
Inches	1¾	2	2	2¼
Stitches	11	12	13	14

Module Size Adult

	S	M	L	1X
Inches	2½	2¾	3	3¼
Stitches	11	12	13	14

——— Cast on
- - - - Pick up and knit
〰〰 Seam
——→ Direction of knitting

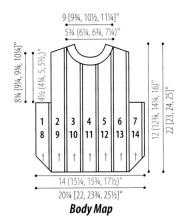

Body Map

CHILD: MC 2 (2, 3, 3) FORTISSIMA Socka 2439
CC 1 (1, 2, 2) FORTISSIMA Sock Yarn 04 shown in size 6;
ADULT: MC 6 (7, 7, 8) NORO Silk Garden 37; CC 5 (5, 6, 6)
Cash Iroha 61 shown on page 73 in size medium

Morgan's Pullover

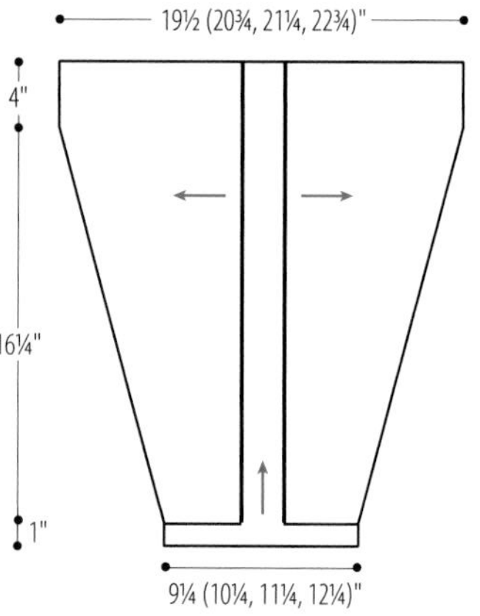

Pick up (61, 65, 75, 85) [76, 80, 84, 88] sts along edge, cast on (8) [15] sts.
Knit 2 rows, purl 1 row, knit 2 rows.

Strip 13
Work as Strip 6 through bind off.
With CC, pick up (66, 70, 80, 90) [88, 92, 96, 100] sts along edge of Strip 6.
Knit 2 rows, purl 1 row, knit 2 rows.
Next row Bind off (25, 27, 31, 35) [35, 37, 39, 41] sts and k the remaining sts. Leave sts on needle — (41, 43, 49, 55) [53, 55, 57, 59] sts.

Strip 14
Work as Strip 7 through bind-off.
With RS facing and CC, pick up (33, 34, 39, 44) [45, 46, 47, 48] sts.
Knit 2 rows, purl 1 row.
Pick up (33, 34, 39, 44) [45, 46, 47, 48] sts along edge of Strip 1. Join to sts on Strip 14 using the 3-needle bind-off with WS of work held together.

SLEEVES (Short for child/long for adult.)
Note Work slipped edge sts along each edge.
With MC and larger needle, cast on 11 (12, 13, 14) sts and work a strip of (3¼, 3¾, 4¼, 4¾)" [20¼]" in Garter Ridge pattern.
With CC, pick up (20, 22, 25, 28) [76] sts along one long edge of strip. * Work (3¼, 3½, 3¾, 4)" [3¼, 3¾, 4¼, 4¾]" in Garter Ridge pattern.
Begin underarm shaping:
Next row (RS) K (18, 20, 23, 26) [72], W&T, work back in pattern.
Next row (RS) K (16, 18, 21, 24) [68], W&T, work back in pattern.
Next row (RS) K (14, 16, 19, 22) [64], W&T, work back in pattern.

Child only
Knit across, hiding wraps. Bind off.
Repeat for other side of Sleeve, reversing shaping.

Adult only
Work as established, working 4 fewer sts each RS row.
After 6 RS rows have been worked, work each of the next 12 RS rows with 3 fewer sts—16 sts.
Next row (RS) K16, W&T, work back in pattern.
Next 2 rows Knit across all 76 sts, hiding wraps. Put these sts on a holder. *

With CC, pick up 76 sts along the other long edge of strip and work * to *, working the W&T on WS rows.

FINISHING
Sew left shoulder seam.
NECKBAND
Row 1 With CC, pick up (89, 95, 101, 107) [116, 122, 128, 134] sts around neck edge.
Row 2 (WS) Knit.
Row 3 With MC, k1, * sl 1 with yarn in back (wyib), k2 repeat from *, end sl 1, k3.
Row 4 Repeat Row 3, with yarn in front (wyif) when slipping sts.
Rows 5 and 6 Repeat Rows 3 and 4.
Rows 7 and 8 With CC, knit.
Rows 9-12 Repeat Rows 3 and 4.
Rows 13 and 14 Knit.
Childs only Bind off.
Adult
Rows 15–18 Repeat Rows 3-6.
Rows 19 and 20 Knit.
Bind off loosely.
Sew right shoulder seam.

CUFF
Work as neckband, over (49, 52, 55, 58) [35, 41, 47, 53] sts.
Sew second shoulder seam.
Sew in sleeves.
Sew underarm seam.
With CC, work 1 row single crochet and 1 row backwards single crochet around bottom edge.
Sew in ends and block lightly.

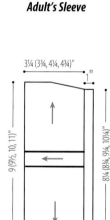

19½ (20¾, 21¼, 22¾)"

4"

16¼"

1"

9¼ (10¼, 11¼, 12¼)"

Adult's Sleeve

3¼ (3¾, 4¼, 4¾)"

1"

9 (9½, 10, 11)"

8¼ (8¾, 9¼, 10¼)"

Child's Sleeve

The **De Colores** jacket is stunning; a graphic pattern and vivid colors almost conceal its simple, strip-at-a-time construction. Instructions follow on the next 2 pages.

De Colores

NOTES

1 See *Techniques*, page 116, for k2tog, ssk, lifted increase, 3-needle bind-off (ridge effect), wrap and turn (W&T), and backwards single crochet. *2* Slip stitches purlwise with yarn at WS of work. *3* If using a variegated yarn, begin each strip at a different point in the colorway than at the beginning of adjoining strips. *4* Use lifted increase throughout pattern.

BASIC STRIP

With B, cast on 20 (22, 24) sts.
Work in chart pattern to length called for in instructions, ending with a RS row unless instructed otherwise. Bind off. Basic Strip measures approximately 4 (4¼, 4¾)" wide when joined to other strips.

BODY

Strips 3LF, 1B, 6B, 1RF
Work Basic Strip to 13½ (15½, 17½)".
Strips 2B and 2RF
Work Basic Strip to 21¼ (23¾, 26½)", ending with a WS row.
Shape shoulder: Short Rows 1, 2 (RS) Work 16 (18, 20) sts, W&T, work to end.
Short Rows 3, 4 Work 12 (14, 16) sts, W&T, work to end.
Short Rows 5, 6 Work 8 (10, 12) sts, W&T, work to end.
Short Rows 7, 8 (WS) Work 4 (6, 8) sts, W&T, work to end.
Row 9 With A, knit, hiding wraps as you come to them. Bind off.
Strips 2LF and 5B
Work as for Strip 2B, reversing shoulder shaping by working short rows on WS rows. On last short row, purl with A, hiding wraps as you come to them.
Strip 3B
Work as for Strip 2B to shoulder shaping.
Shape neck: Next Row (RS) Bind off 11 sts (neck edge), work to end. Continue to bind off at neck edge 2 sts twice, 1 st once—4 (6, 8) sts. Work 2 rows even. Bind off with A.
Strip 4B
Work as for Strip 3B, reversing neck shaping by binding off at beginning of WS rows.
Strip 3RF
Work Basic Strip to 13½ (15½, 17½)", ending with a WS row.

Shape V-neck: Row 1 (RS) With A, k1, sl 1, work in pattern as established to end.
Row 2 Work to last 2 sts, end sl 2.
Row 3 With B, k1, ssk, work in pattern to end.
Row 4 Work to last 2 sts, p1, sl 1. [Repeat Rows 1–4] 15 times more—4 (6, 8) sts. Work 21 rows even. Bind off.
Strip 1LF
Work as for Strip 3RF, reversing neck shaping as follows:
Row 1 (RS) With A, work in pattern to last 2 sts, sl 1, k1.
Row 2 Sl 2, work to end.
Row 3 Work to last 3 sts, k2tog, k1.
Row 4 Sl 1, p1, work to end.

SLEEVES

Strips 2S and 3S
Work Basic Strip to 18¼ (20¾, 23¼)".
Strip 1S
Work Basic Strip to 4½ (5¼, 6¼)", ending with a WS row.
Begin decreases: Row 1 (RS) With B, work in pattern to last 3 sts, k2tog, k1.
Rows 2, 6 Sl 1, p1, work to end.
Rows 3, 7 With A, work to last 2 sts, sl 1, k1.
Rows 4, 8 Sl 2, work to end.
Row 5 With B, work to last 2 sts, k2. [Repeat Rows 1–8] 14 (16, 18) times more, then work Rows 1–6 once more—4 sts. Bind off.
Strip 4S
Work as for Strip 1S, reversing shaping as follows:
Row 1 (RS) With B, k1, ssk, work to end.
Rows 2, 6 Work to last 2 sts, p1, sl 1.
Rows 3, 7 With A, k1, sl 1, work to end.
Rows 4, 8 Work to last 2 sts, sl 2.
Row 5 With B, k2, work to end.

FINISHING

Block strips to measurements. Join each strip to its neighbor, following the Map: With RS facing, circular needle and A, pick up and k1 st in each slip st along edge. Set this needle aside. With separate needle, pick up along edge of adjoining strip. Hold strips with WS together, then beginning at lower edge, join sts using 3-needle bind-off. When joining shorter underarm strips of Body to longer strips,

Gradations of color serve as a background for the black maze-like mosaic pattern of this strip-knit jacket. The detachable collar and reversible (double-sided) button dress the jacket up or down according to your mood.

continue to bind off sts up armhole edge on longer strips after all sts from shorter strips are used. When joining Strips 2 and 3 on Sleeves, and underarm strips on Body, bind off first 2" (of Sleeves) and 4" (of Body) of each strip separately before joining strips with 3-needle bind-off. Sew shoulders. Sew top of Sleeves to straight edges of armholes. Sew straight portion at top of Sleeves to bound-off armhole sts. Sew Sleeve seams.

Lower back crocheted band

With crochet hook and A, work 3 rows single crochet (sc) and 1 row backwards sc along lower edge of Back, from side slit to side slit.

Front and neckband

With crochet hook and A, work crocheted band along lower edge of right front, up center front, along back neck, down left center front, and along lower edge of left front. Work increases at each corner (by working twice into 1 st) on Rows 1 and 3. Work 2 buttonholes on Row 2 (by working chain 3 in place of 1 sc), 1 on each front edge just below point where neck shaping starts. To create reversible Jacket button, attach 2 decorative buttons to each other using wire or strong thread; place through left front buttonhole.

Sleeve cuff band

Work crocheted band along lower edge of Sleeves, beginning and ending at slit.

OPTIONAL REMOVABLE COLLAR

With B, cast on 95 sts.

Rows 1, 3 (RS) Purl.

Row 2 (Buttonhole row) K3, * yo, k2tog, k7, [yo, k2tog, k8] twice, yo, k2tog, k7 *, [yo, k2tog, k4] twice, repeat from * to * once, yo, k2tog, k2.

Row 4 Knit.

Row 5 K32, place marker (pm), k15, pm, k1, pm, k15, pm, knit to end.

Row 6 Knit.

Row 7 Knit to first marker, increase in next st, knit to 1 st before 2nd marker, increase in next st, k1, increase in next st, knit to 1 st before last marker, increase in next st, knit to last 3 sts, W&T.

Row 8 Knit to last 3 sts of row, W&T. Continue working increases at markers every RS row (4 sts increased), AT SAME TIME, continue short rows as follows:

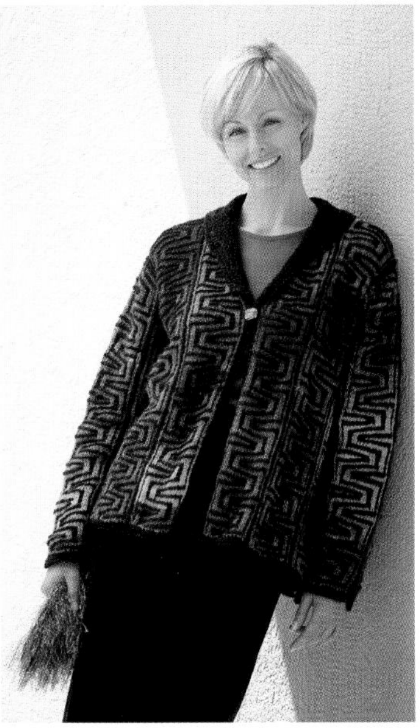

Next 2 rows Work to last 6 sts of row, W&T.

Next 2 rows Work to last 9 sts of row, W&T.

Next 2 rows Work to 10 sts, W&T.

Next 2 rows Work to last 11 sts, W&T.

Next 2 rows Work to last 12 sts, W&T.

Next 2 rows Work to last 13 sts, W&T. Cut yarn. Slip all sts to LH needle.

Next row Knit. Bind off loosely but do not cut yarn; place remaining st onto crochet hook and work 2 rows sc, then 1 row backwards sc.

Sew buttons along inside of Jacket neck to correspond to Collar buttonholes.

Noro Cash Iroha 10 (11, 12) balls color 2 black (A)
Silk Garden 7 (7, 8) balls color 50 (B); shown in Medium

Strip Width

	S	M	L
Inches	4	4¼	4¾
Stitches	20	22	24

Small

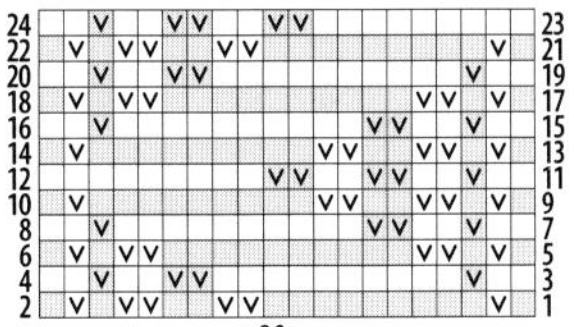

20 sts

Medium

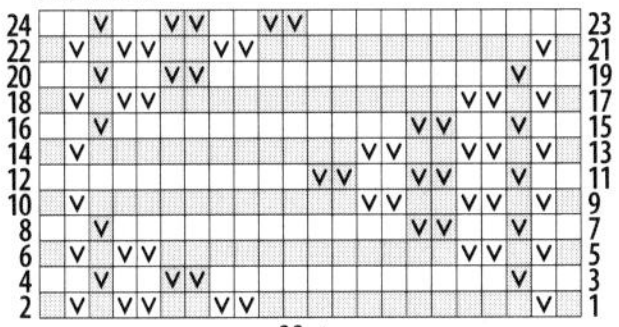

22 sts

Large

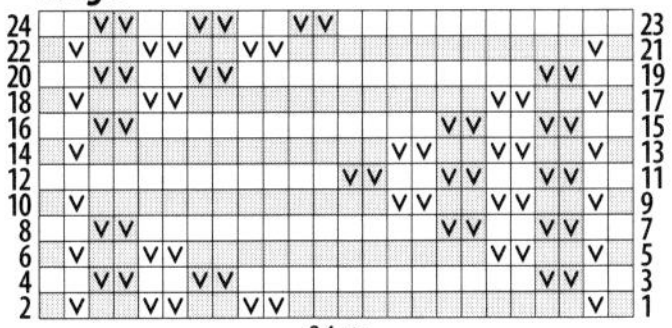

24 sts

Stitch Key

- *Garter st (k on RS and WS)*
- *Stockinette st (k on RS and p on WS)*
- V *Sl 1 purlwise with yarn at WS of work*

Color Key

- *A*
- *B*

Chart Note

Work chart as a mosaic pattern. Each chart row is worked twice: reading from right to left for a right-side (odd-numbered) row and from left to right for a wrong-side (even-numbered) row. Each chart row is worked with one color of yarn, alternating 2 rows of color A with 2 rows of color B. The first stitch of the chart row indicates the color to be worked on that row; all stitches of the other color are slipped (purlwise and with yarn on WS).

Join with 3-needle bind-off (ridge effect)
Edges are not joined
Direction of knitting

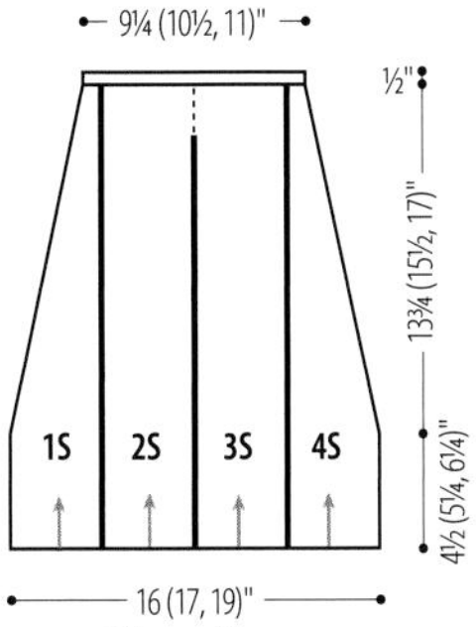
9¼ (10½, 11)"
½"
13¾ (15½, 17)"
4½ (5¼, 6¼)"
1S
2S
3S
4S
16 (17, 19)"

Sleeve Map

Body Map

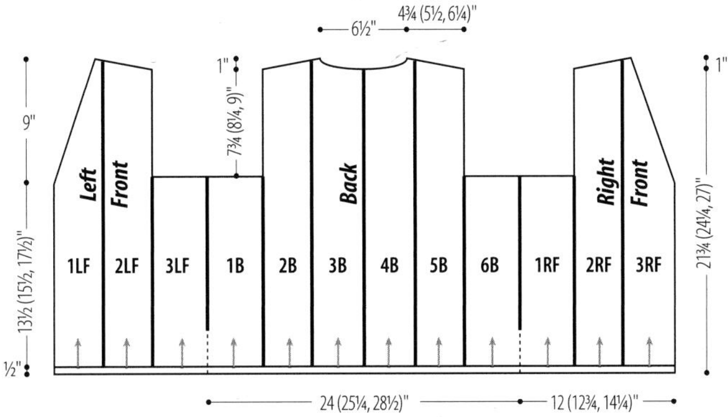
6½"
4¾ (5½, 6¼)"
1"
7¾ (8¼, 9)"
9"
13½ (15½, 17½)"
½"
1"
21¾ (24¼, 27)"
Left Front
Back
Right Front
1LF
2LF
3LF
1B
2B
3B
4B
5B
6B
1RF
2RF
3RF
24 (25¼, 28½)"
12 (12¾, 14¼)"

patchwork

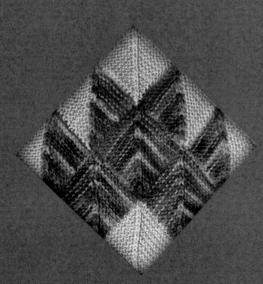

patchwork

Our rich heritage of patchwork quilt patterns provides an invaluable source of ideas for knitting designs. Although I'm not a quilter, my library contains numerous quilt books. The fact that a single design can have so many different appearances (depending on the placement of light and dark colors) continually fascinates me.

Let's focus on geometric quilt designs composed of shapes we already know how to knit: squares, triangles, and rectangles. Two simple patchwork designs, Log Cabin (rectangles) and Flying Geese (right triangles) demonstrate how a single shape can be repeated to create appealing, easy-to-knit motifs.

While some of the knitting in the early chapters was random and freeform—knit a square or rectangle of any size, bind off, pick up stitches along any edge and knit with a new yarn—the approach must be more disciplined to reproduce quilt patterns. Having a plan, drawn on a computer or the grid paper on pages 114 and 115 is the easiest way to proceed. Once the stitch gauge is determined, the drawing can serve as the pattern.

As with other modular knitting, geometric patchwork blocks can be used as entire sweater fronts and backs, as accents (pockets or patches on the body and sleeves), or to make accessories such as tablemats, pillows, and bags.

The construction of knitted quilt blocks is the same as for sewn fabric blocks, except that the individual shapes are knit rather than cut from fabric. Once one section of the quilt block is knit, stitches are picked up along an edge for the next piece.

Let's look at some quilt block designs and consider how to knit them. I'll show you how these designs can be incorporated into garments and other knit projects, and present examples of how to use them as a starting point for original designs.

FLYING GEESE

I've always loved the Flying Geese quilt pattern. Constructed of three triangles, the block can be bold and colorful, or subtle and understated, according to the colors used. Color placement is up to you, but I usually use the dominant color for the large triangle.

To knit a Flying Geese block, begin by casting on an odd number of stitches for the base of the large triangle. An odd number of stitches results in a sharper point at the top of the triangle. Then knit a right-angle triangle that begins with the hypotenuse. In garter stitch (or garter ridge), decrease on each edge every other row; in stockinette stitch, decrease on each edge, 3 of every 4 rows.

When this large triangle is completed, change colors and pick up stitches along one of its short edges for a small triangle. To determine the number of stitches to pick up, divide the number of stitches cast on for the large triangle by 1.4 (for example, if 21 were cast on, pick up 15). Work the small triangle the same as the large one.

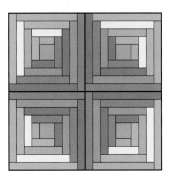

The Log Cabin block is introduced on page 13; 4-block motif

Knitting the Flying Geese block

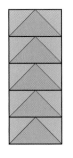
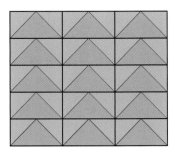

Stack blocks for strips; join strips for wider pieces

An 8-motif square

Reverse colors for a chevron

How would you knit these patterns?

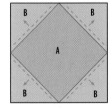

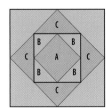

Building a Diamond-in-a-Square block

When the small triangle is complete, pick up the the same number of stitches along the other short edge of the large triangle and work a second small triangle.

These 3 triangles form one Flying Geese block, a rectangle that is twice as long as it is high. One way to combine multiple blocks is to stack them. To do this, pick up stitches (the same number of stitches that were cast on for the large triangle) along the top of the completed block. Repeat the process of knitting the 3 triangles to build another block. Continuing stacking as many blocks as desired to make a long strip of Flying Geese. Join strips for a wider fabric.

VARIATIONS

Flying Geese blocks can be arranged in other ways. Because the block is twice as wide as it is high, a stack of 2 blocks creates a square. To build on the square, rotate it 90 degrees, pick up stitches along the edge and knit 2 more stacked blocks to form a second square. Turn this piece 90 degrees, knit 2 more blocks, then make another 90-degree turn and knit 2 more. The result is one large square made of 8 Flying Geese blocks.

By reversing the placement of dark and light colors, interesting visual effects can be achieved. Two stacked Flying Geese blocks with the colors of the large and small triangles reversed create the illusion of a chevron shape. These chevrons also can be arranged in a long strip, or rotated to form a large square.

There are many other ways in which single blocks or panels of blocks can be joined and rotated to create unique designs. The Flying Geese block can also be combined with solid-color squares or rectangles.

DIAMOND IN A SQUARE

Another traditional quilt block design that is easy to knit is Diamond in a Square. Begin by knitting a square (A), then pick up stitches (the same number as cast on) along one edge of the square. Knit a right triangle (B) with decreases on each edge, just as for the Flying Geese block. Repeat on the other 3 edges of the square.

After the 4 triangles are completed, knit another group of 4 right triangles (C). Begin the first C triangle by picking up stitches along the short edges of 2 B triangles.
- To determine the number of stitches to pick up along this edge, divide the number of stitches in the base of triangle B (the same the number cast on for square A) by 1.4; for example, 21 sts ÷ 1.4 = 15 sts.
- The result is the number of stitches in the short edge of triangle B.
- Double that number to get the number of stitches for the base of triangle C: 15 sts × 2 = 30 sts. Subtract 1 stitch for an odd number of stitches.

patchwork

VIRGINIA REEL (OR MONKEY WRENCH OR SNAIL'S TRAIL)

I didn't realize that the same quilt pattern might have several names until I knit the Virginia Reel and a friend came up to me and said, "I see you've knit a Snail's Trail!" I learned the same pattern is also referred to as Monkey Wrench.

Viewed from a distance, this pattern appears to be composed of curving forms, but when seen up close or on grid paper, it is achieved by cleverly arranged squares and triangles. The optical illusion arises from the placement of light and dark colors.

The schematic shows the sections numbered in the order in which they are knit. Two strongly contrasting colors or groups of colors are used (one light and the other dark) and worked alternately throughout. Begin by casting on for square 1 with the light color. Knit the square and bind off. Turn 90 degrees and with a dark color, pick up the same number of stitches and work square 2. Bind off, turn 90 degrees and knit a square with a light color. Turn and knit square 4 with a dark color. Seam the side edge of square 4 to the cast-on edge of square 1. (Although you could join these edges as you knit, I usually sew this seam afterwards, to make the joined edges of all 4 squares look identical.)

The rest of the Virginia Reel block is constructed in series of 4 triangles, just as in the Diamond-in-a-Square block. The number of stitches in the base of the first triangle (section 5) is twice the number of stitches in one of the small squares (minus 1, if necessary, to make the base of the triangle an odd number of stitches). For example, if there were 10 stitches in each square, double this to get 20 stitches, then subtract one and use 19 stitches as the base of triangle 5. You will continue to alternate light and dark: square 4 was dark, so for triangle 5, pick up stitches along the side of 4 and the next square (1) with light. The colors alternate in the remaining three triangles in this round.

Just as with the Diamond in a Square, you can continue knitting larger and larger triangles until the piece is the desired size. Use the same calculation as for Diamond in a Square to determine the number of stitches in the short sides of new triangles. At the beginning of each set of 4 triangles, be sure to check the placement of the light and dark colors, maintaining the light-dark-light-dark sequence throughout. Otherwise, you may end up with an interesting design, but it won't be the intriguing spiral of the Virginia Reel.

Several blocks can be joined to create a larger, interlocking design. Rotate alternate blocks by 90° before joining them to create an interesting pattern that appears to flow from one section to the next.

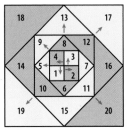

Building a Virginia Reel block

Join blocks

Rotate, then join

Other quilt patterns

Louisiana

Maple Leaf

Windmill

Sailboat

Star

My approach to Formal Garden

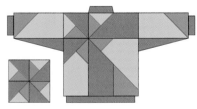
Pinwheel motif sweater

ANALYZING QUILT PATTERNS

Most quilt blocks could be knit in several different ways. Formal Garden is a good example. After devising several ways to knit this quilt pattern, some of which were rather involved, I suddenly saw that this pattern could easily be constructed of 4 right triangles, each begun with the short edge, in a dark color, then changed to a light color about a third of the way through.

I love to go through quilt books, analyzing how I would knit the blocks. Often it is a trial-and-error process, where I say to myself, "Now what if I cast on here and knit this shape, then picked up here and knit this piece?" Sometimes it doesn't work out, and I begin again at another place in the design. Most of these pieces never get knit (because there is never enough time!) but the mental process of figuring out the most logical way to knit the pattern is fun and satisfying in itself. Drawing the pattern on our grid paper (page 114) can help you see the possibilities.

QUILTS AS A STARTING POINT

As appealing as many quilt block patterns are, I don't usually want to reproduce a particular motif. Instead, it serves as a starting point for an original design. I usually photocopy the quilt block, then make several rough sketches of possible patterns. When I develop something that shows promise, I'll draw it out in more detail, often on grid paper or on the computer.

One such design began with a quilt block named Pinwheel. This block is fun to knit, but it can have the appearance of a bull's eye, something I don't want on the front of my garment. I decided to put the block design on the shoulder of a pullover sweater, letting the different colors flow from the triangles out onto the rest of the sweater. The basic quilt block design is knit first, and then the solid-colored areas are picked up and knit.

If you enjoy these quilt patterns, take a look at patchwork pattern books and try to visualize how you would knit the blocks. See if any of them give you ideas for developing your own designs.

PATTERNS

The Star Block used in Star Light, Star Bright, page 92, is a color variation of the Windmill block. Kalapaki Bay, page 94, is a bold, garter-ridge interpretation of the Diamond in a Square.

patchwork

Darn it!
There's a hole
in my block.

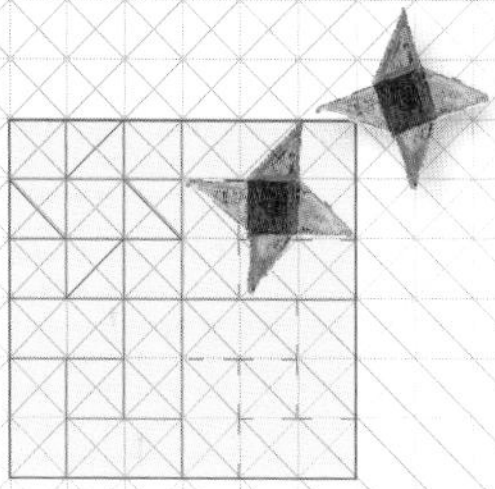

Star Light, p. 92

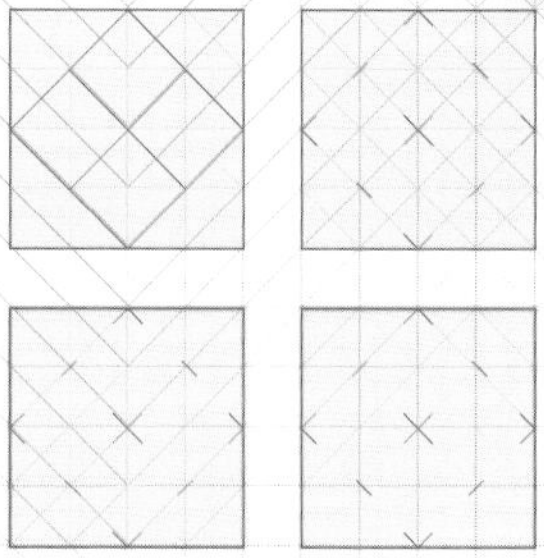

Kalpaki Bay, p. 94

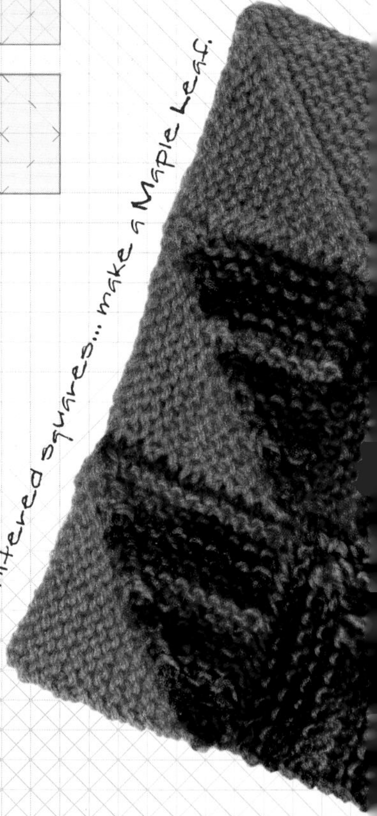

WORK IT OUT

The grid on page 114 is
especially helpful when
mixing shapes.

Kids love
color— here is
a chance to play.

5 mitered squares... make a Maple Leaf.

SWATCH TRICKS

Reversing or rotating
light and dark colors can
greatly change the look of
a patchwork pattern.

Complicated? Not really.
It's just 2 squares,
2 triangles—
2 sizes of each.

Star Light, Star Bright

Experienced

OVERSIZED FIT

8 (10, 12)

Measures approximately
A 34 (36, 38)"
B 17½ (17¾, 18½)"
C 22½ (23½, 24½)"

10cm/4"

over Garter Ridge Pattern,
using larger needles and double
strands of yarn

1 2 3 **4** 5 6

Medium weight

MC 475 (550, 600) yds teal
A 280 (305, 330) yds yellow
B 105 (115, 125) yds purple
C 45 (50, 55) yds garnet

3.5 and 3.75mm/US 4 and 5
or size to obtain gauge

Stitch holders and markers
Spare circular needle of required
size for 3-needle bind-off

MUENCH Marathon (2
strands held together) 4 (5,
5) skeins 44 (MC); 3 (3, 3)
skeins 53 (A); 1 (1, 2) skeins
51 (B); 1 (1, 1) skeins 107
(C); shown on page 85 in
size 8

NOTES

1 See *Techniques*, page 116, for ssk, ssp, 3-needle bind-off (ridge effect), and wrap and turn (W&T). **2** In these instructions, "pick up" means "pick up and knit." Pick up all stitches with RS facing. **3** When changing colors, bring new color under old to prevent holes. **4** Slip all stitches purlwise with yarn to WS. **5** Refer to Map for cast-on or pick-up, direction of work, edges to be sewn, and placement of squares.

GARTER RIDGE PATTERN

Rows 1, 3 (RS) Knit.
Row 2 Knit.
Row 4 Purl.
Repeat Rows 1–4 for pattern.

BASIC PINWHEEL MOTIF (make 8)
Center Square

With larger needles and C, cast on 12 sts and work in seed st as follows:
Row 1 * K1, p1; repeat from * across row.
Row 2 Purl the knit sts and knit the purl sts.
Repeat Rows 1 and 2 for 14 rows total.
Bind off. Set aside.

Section 1

Row 1 With larger needles and A, cast on 12 (or pick up depending on where you are on the Map) sts.
Row 2 (WS) Knit 1 row.
Work 14 more rows in St st (knit on RS, purl on WS), slipping first st of every RS row as if to purl. With B, pick up 12 sts along one edge of the center square. Place marker, pick up A and knit across 12 sts—24 sts.
Work a 2-color mitered square in St st, decreasing in 3 of every 4 rows, beginning with next purl row:
WS rows With A, purl to 2 sts before marker, ssp, drop A; with B, p2tog, purl to end.
RS rows With B, knit to 2 sts before marker, k2tog; with A, ssk, knit to end.
When 2 sts remain, p2tog, fasten off.

Section 2

Work as Section 1, EXCEPT join WS rows to previous section by p2tog (last st with edge st of previous section).
Sections 3, 4 Work as Section 2. Sew Section 4 to Section 1. Motif measures approximately 6" × 6".

4- PINWHEEL UNIT

Unit measures approximately 13" × 13".
* With C, pick up 30 sts along edge of one pinwheel. Knit 1 row. Change to MC, knit 1 row. Set aside. Repeat from * with another pinwheel. Join pinwheels using MC and 3-needle bind-off. Repeat with 2 more pinwheels. Join 2-pinwheel strips, picking up 68 sts along each long edge. Repeat from * with 4 remaining pinwheels.
** With larger needles and C, pick up 68 sts across top of one 4-pinwheel unit. Knit 1 row; put sts on holder. Repeat across from ** for bottom of unit.

RIGHT UNDERARM PANEL

With larger needles and C, pick up 1 st from sts on hold at bottom or top edge, 66 sts along side of unit, and 1 st from other holder—68 sts. Knit 1 row. With MC, knit 2 rows. Bind off 20 sts; work 12 (16, 20) rows Garter Ridge Pattern on 48 sts. Bind off.

LEFT UNDERARM PANEL

Work as right Underarm Panel, EXCEPT begin picking up at bottom edge and reverse shaping.

BOTTOM BAND

Note Slip all stitches with yarn to WS.
Row 1 With larger needle and MC, pick up 9 (11, 13) sts along bottom of underarm panel, knit 76 sts from holder, and pick up 9 (11, 13) sts along bottom of other underarm panel—94 (98, 102) sts.
Row 2 Knit.
Rows 3, 4 With B, knit 1 row, purl 1 row.
Row 5 With A, * k2, sl 2; repeat from *, end k2.
Row 6 Repeat Row 5.
Row 7 With B, k4, sl 2, * k2, sl 2; repeat from *, end k4.
Row 8 With B, p4, sl 2, * p2, sl 2; repeat from *, end p4.
Repeat Rows 5–8 one (2, 3) more time(s).
With smaller needles and B, knit 4 rows. Bind off loosely.
Repeat on the other 4-Pinwheel Unit.

BACK YOKE

Row 1 (RS) With larger needle and MC, pick up 1 st along top of underarm panel, knit 68 sts from

The cheerful star-like motif on this child's sweater is both fun and challenging to knit. Because of the complexity involved in knitting the star motifs, this sweater is sized in the side panels and top yoke section.

holder, pick up 1 st along top of underarm panel—70 sts.

Row 2 Knit.

Beginning with Row 3, work 10 (14, 18) rows Garter Ridge Pattern.

Right Back Neck Shaping

Row 1 (RS) Knit.

Row 2 Knit 26 and put these sts on a holder, bind off 18, knit to end.

Row 3 Knit.

Short Rows 4, 5 Bind off 3 sts, p19, wrap and turn (W&T), knit to end.

Short Rows 6, 7 Bind off 2 sts, k11, W&T, knit to end.

Short Rows 8, 9 Bind off 1 st, p5, W&T, knit to end.

Row 10 Knit across all sts, picking up and knitting short-row wraps—20 sts; place on holder.

Repeat for left Back neck with the 26 sts that are on hold, reversing shaping.

FRONT YOKE

Begin as Back Yoke, EXCEPT work 2 (6, 10) rows Garter Ridge Pattern before shaping.

Left Front Neck Shaping

Row 1 and all RS rows Knit.

Row 2 (WS) K29 and put these sts on a holder, bind off 12, knit to end.

* Continue in Garter Ridge Pattern AT SAME TIME, at beginning of WS rows, bind off 3 sts once, 2 sts twice, and 1 st once—25 sts.

Short Rows 12, 13 Bind off 1 st, p16, W&T, knit to end.

Short Rows 14, 15 K11, W&T, knit to end.

Short Rows 16, 17 P5, W&T, knit to end.

Row 18 Knit across all sts, picking up and knitting short-row wraps—20 sts; place on holder.

Repeat from * for right Front neck, reversing shaping. Join left Front and left Back shoulders with MC and 3-needle bind-off.

NECK BAND

Row 1 With larger needle, B, and beginning at right shoulder, pick up 9 sts along right Back neck, 17 sts across Back neck, 9 sts to left shoulder, 14 sts along left Front neck, 12 sts across Front neck, and 14 sts to right shoulder—75 sts.

Beginning with Row 2, work as Bottom Band through Row 15. Bind off.

— Cast on
- - - Pick up and knit
···· P2tog join
wwww Seam
→ Direction of knitting

Center square

Start Section 1 with a square

Pick up stitches along center square and complete Section 1 with a mitered square

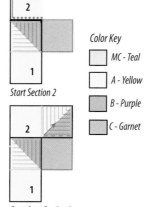

Start Section 2

Complete Section 2

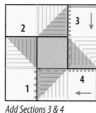

Add Sections 3 & 4

Pinwheel Map

Color Key
- MC - Teal
- A - Yellow
- B - Purple
- C - Garnet

Join right Front and Back shoulders with MC and 3-needle bind-off.

SLEEVES

Row 1 With larger needle and MC, cast on 70 (75, 80) sts.

Row 2 Knit.

Short-row shaping

Short Rows 3, 4 K12 (15, 18), W&T, purl to end.

Short Rows 5, 6 K17 (20, 23), W&T, knit to end.

Short Rows 7, 8 K22, (25, 28), W&T, purl to end.

Continue in Garter Ridge Pattern, knitting 5 more sts every RS row, until all sts are knit. Work 48 (56, 60) rows on all sts.

Next Short Rows K67 (70, 73) W&T, knit to end.

Continue, reversing short-row shaping by knitting 5 fewer sts every RS row, ending with last pair of short rows: k12 (15, 18), W&T, purl to end.

Next Row Knit across all sts. Bind off.

CUFFS

Row 1 With larger needle and MC, pick up 38 (42, 46) sts along bottom edge of Sleeve. Beginning with Row 2, work as Bottom Band. With larger needle, bind off.

FINISHING

Block. Sew top of Sleeves to armhole, lining up center Garter Ridge with shoulder seam and matching ridges. Sew straight part of Sleeve sides to underarm edge. Sew Sleeve seams. Sew side seam of neckband on RS so that the ridge will not show when it rolls.

Sew in ends.

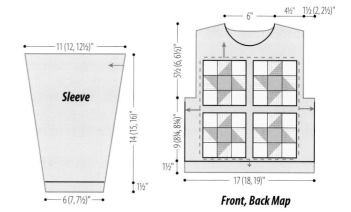

Sleeve

11 (12, 12½)"

14 (15, 16)"

1½"

6 (7, 7½)"

6" — 4½" — 1½ (2, 2½)"

5½ (6, 6½)"

9 (8¾, 8¼)"

1½"

17 (18, 19)"

Front, Back Map

Kalapaki Bay

Intermediate

One Size
Measures approximately 32" x 45"

10cm/4"

38 | *GET CLOSE*

20

over garter ridge pattern

1 2 **3** 4 5 6

Light weight
MC *675 yds*
A *310 yds*
B *230 yds*
C *280 yds*
D *130 yds*

4mm/US 6
or size to obtain gauge

Size 3.75/F

&

Spare needle for 3-needle bind-off

NOTES
1 See *Techniques*, page 116, for ssk, S2KP2, 3-needle bind-off, single and backwards crochet. *2* In these instructions, "pick up" means "pick up and knit." Pick up all stitches with RS facing. *3* Slip stitches as if to purl, with yarn to wrong side of work. *4* Refer to Maps for placement of Squares, Triangles, and Rectangles; and direction of work.

Garter Ridge Pattern
Rows 1 and 3 (RS) Knit.
Row 2 Knit.
Row 4 Purl.
Repeat Rows 1–4 for pattern.

DIAMOND-IN-A-SQUARE-BLOCK (make 12)
Beginning with Square 1 and following the numbers on the Map, work Squares, Triangles, and Rectangles as follows:

Square 1
Row 1 (RS) With MC, cast on 25 sts (12+1+12).
Row 2 Knit.
Rows 3, 5 Knit to 1 st before center st, S2KP2, knit to end.
Row 4 Purl.
Row 6 Knit to center st, p1, knit to end.
Repeat Rows 3–6 until 3 sts remain.
Next row (RS) Work S2KP2, fasten off.
Square 2
Row 1 With MC, cast on 13 sts, pick up 12 sts along one edge of Square 1.
Work as Square 1, beginning with Row 2.
Square 3
Work as Square 2, EXCEPT pick up along Square 2.
Square 4
Row 1 With MC, pick up 12 sts along Square 1, 1 st at corner of Square 2, 12 sts along Square 3.
Work as Square 1, beginning with Row 2.
Triangles 5–8
Row 1 (RS) With A, pick up 24 sts as shown on Map.
Row 2 Knit.
Rows 3, 5 K1, ssk, knit to last 3 sts, k2tog, k1.
Row 4 Purl.
Row 6 Knit.
Repeat Rows 3–6 until 4 sts remain.
Next row (RS) Ssk, k2tog.

Next row Purl.
Next row K2tog, fasten off.
Rectangles 9, 10
Row 1 (RS) With B, pick up 34 sts as shown on Map. Work 9 rows Garter Ridge Pattern, beginning with Row 2. Bind off.
Rectangles 11, 12
With C, pick up 46 sts (6 along each rectangle and 17 along each triangle), as shown on Map. Work as Rectangles 9 and 10. Bind off.
Block Square to 9¼".

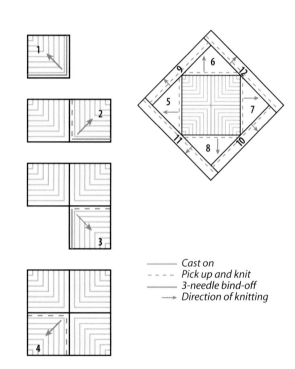

—— Cast on
– – – Pick up and knit
—— 3-needle bind-off
→ Direction of knitting

ASSEMBLY
3-Block Strip
** With D, pick up 45 sts along the purple edge of one block. Knit 1 row.
Next 2 rows With MC, * k1, sl 1; repeat from * across row, end k1.
Next 3 rows Knit. Place sts on spare needle. **
Repeat from ** to ** along the green edge of another block, then join these two blocks with the 3-needle bind-off.

This throw was designed and knit while I was on the beautiful island of Kauai, Hawaii, overlooking Kalapaki Bay. This stunning throw is composed of twelve Diamond-in-a-Square quilt blocks. You could easily add more blocks to increase the size.

Repeat from ** to ** on the other green edge of the second block above, then on the purple edge of another block, and join with 3-needle bind-off. This completes one 3-block strip. Make another strip just like it.

Make two more strips with the green and purple edges reversed (begin by picking up 45 sts along the green edge of one block).

Join Strips

Join the four strips together along their long edges in the same way, picking up 145 sts. Alternate the strips as shown on the Map.

Edging

With D, pick up 145 sts along one end of throw. Knit 1 row.

Next 2 rows With MC,* k1, sl 1; repeat from *, end k1.

Knit 6 rows. Bind off.

Work Edging at other end of throw. With MC and crochet hook, work 1 row single crochet and 1 row backwards crochet around outside edge of throw.

Sew in ends and block lightly.

HEIRLOOM YARNS Easy Care 8 Wool 7 skeins wine 750 (MC); 4 skeins light gray 797 (A); 3 skeins each plum 779 (B) and green 792 (C); 2 skeins thistle 771 (D)

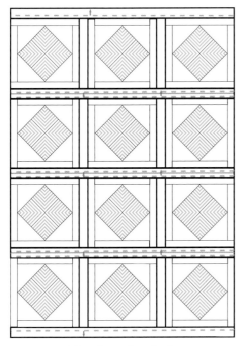

Join strips and work edge

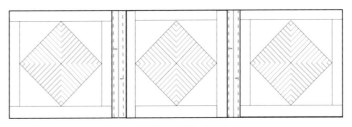

Assembling 3-block strip

bias knitting

bias knitting

Diagonal lines are dynamic and exciting. They add interest and drama to nearly any composition, whether it is an oil painting or a sweater front. These lines are flattering to most figure types, drawing the eye upward and focusing attention on the face and shoulders. Thus, clothing designers often incorporate diagonals into their creations. Let's look at ways to create diagonals in modular knitting.

BIAS STRIPS

One of the easiest ways to create diagonals lines is by knitting bias strips. These strips can be wide or narrow, patterned or solid. They can be used as bands and trims on sweaters and other knit items, or they can be joined together to create entire sweater fronts and other large fabric pieces.

For a garter-stitch strip, begin by casting on enough stitches for the diagonal line of the strip. (How many would that be? If you know how wide you want the strip to be, that measurement is the base of an imaginary right triangle. Find the hypoteneuse by multiplying the base by 1.4. The result is the number of stitches to cast on for the bias strip.) Knit back across the wrong side of the work. Increase 1 stitch at the beginning and decrease 1 stitch at the end of every right-side row. Work wrong-side rows even. Rows worked in this manner are on the diagonal as the piece grows longer. Knit until the strip is the desired length, and bind off.

INCREASES AND DECREASES

I usually move the increases and decreases one stitch in from the edge for a neat, clean edge. I use the k2tog decrease on right-slanting edges and the ssk decrease on left-slanting edges. Increases can be worked using any of several techniques, depending on the situation. I usually increase by knitting into the stitch below (lifted increase), to avoid tightening the edge. Sometimes I use kf&b (knit into the front and back of the stitch) or Make 1 increases (for details, see page 118).

SQUARED-OFF ENDS

The bias strip I just described begins and ends with a point. For a bias strip with a squared-off base, cast on 3 stitches, knit back across the wrong side, then increase 1 stitch at each end of every right-side row until the bottom edge reaches the desired width (see the Sonata shawl on page 103). To square off the top edge, decrease 1 stitch at each end of every right-side row until 3 stitches remain. Knit 3 together, cut the yarn and pull it through the remaining stitch.

STOCKINETTE BIAS STRIP

A stockinette-stitch bias strip is worked the same way, except increase (and decrease) on 3 of every 4 rows, rather than every other row.

YARN CHOICE AND COLOR PLACEMENT

The yarns you choose for your bias strips will control the visual effect. Hand-dyed yarns yield interesting patterning, which varies with the dyeing technique. Short color repeats will produce striped or spotted strips; longer stretches of color will form small blocks or parallelograms.

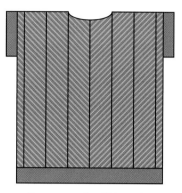

Sweater made of bias strips

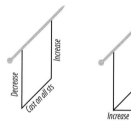

Cast on all stitches for a bias strip or just a few to square the base

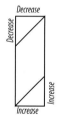

Squaring the top and bottom of a bias strip

Add stripes of varied widths

Or add stripes of 2 rows each

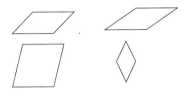

A bias variation

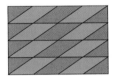

Parallelograms

*All-over parallelogram
pattern*

45° angle

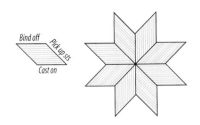

Shape more frequently   *Or less frequently*

Solid-colored yarns can be knit in color blocks or in stripes of any width. One of the most effective stripe patterns for bias strips is 2 rows of one color, then 2 rows of another. Alternate 2 colors, or add additional colors to the sequence. Add interest by varying the width of the stripes.

BIAS STRIP VARIATION
Cast on 3 stitches and increase on one edge only until the piece is the desired width. In garter stitch, knit back across the wrong side, then increase on the left edge of every right-side row. When the strip is the desired width, decrease 1 stitch on the right edge and increase 1 stitch on the left edge of every right-side row. When the strip is the desired length, continue to decrease 1 stitch on the right edge of every right-side row, but do not increase. For stockinette stitch, increase or decrease on 3 of every 4 rows.

PARALLELOGRAMS
A parallelogram is a four-sided figure in which opposite sides are parallel to each other and the same length. Squares and rectangles are parallelograms, as are bias strips. They can be striped, patterned, or worked in blocks of solid colors. They can be all the same size and orientation, or they can vary in both aspects.

As for bias strips, increases are worked on one edge and decreases on the other edge. The frequency of increases and decreases determines the acuteness of the angles, and thus the shape of the knitted piece. If the shaping is worked every other row in garter stitch or 3 of every 4 rows in stockinette stitch, it produces 45° angles. Shape more frequently to produce sharper angles, less frequently for less acute angles.

A PARALLELOGRAM STAR
It's easy to build 45°-angle parallelograms into an 8-pointed star shape. Cast on stitches for the base of one parallelogram, for example, 20 stitches. Working in garter stitch, knit back across these 20 stitches, creating the first garter ridge. Knit 38 more rows, decreasing at the beginning and increasing at the end of every right-side row, changing color every 2 rows. Bind off. There will be 20 striped garter stitch ridges in this piece.

Now, with color A, pick up 20 stitches (the same number cast on for the first piece) along the decrease edge of the first piece and knit another piece just like the first. Repeat 6 more times, for a total of 8 parallelograms. Sew the edge of the last piece to the cast-on edge of the first. This basic design could have solid blocks of color instead of the stripes. It could be a tablemat, or a motif on a sweater or throw.

bias knitting

CHEVRONS

The chevron's flattering lines draw the eye up to the face and shoulders. You already know how to knit a chevron shape using two parallelograms, one a mirror image of the other (just decrease at the beginning and increase at the end of the rows). However, it is easy to knit the two parallelograms at the same time and create this shape in one piece.

BASIC CHEVRON

Begin by casting on the stitches for the bottom edge of one parallelogram (A-B in our drawing), 1 extra stitch for the center decrease line, then the stitches for the base of the other parallelogram (B-C). Knit or purl back across the wrong side. In garter stitch, increase 1 stitch at the beginning of each right-side row, knit until 1 stitch before the center stitch, work a 3-to-1 decrease (I prefer S2KP2), knit to the left edge and increase 1 stitch. On wrong-side rows, knit across, except purl the center stitch.

Adjust the rate of increase and decrease to the stitch pattern: in stockinette stitch, work the increases and decreases on 3 of every 4 rows.

SQUARED-OFF CHEVRON

For a chevron with a square bottom edge, begin working each corner separately, just as for the bias strip. When one edge of the knitting is half the desired width of the chevron, set this piece aside and make another one just like it. To join the two pieces together, knit across the right side of one piece, cast on 1 center stitch and knit across the stitches of the other piece. Continue just as for the basic chevron.

To finish off the top edge of the chevron, there are 2 options. Bind off all stitches when the side edges are the desired length. This produces a deep V shape that follows the lines of the chevron. Or, switch from increasing to decreasing, which will create a straight line across the top of the piece. Continue to work the center decreases as before until 7 stitches remain. Then ssk, S2KP2, k2tog. Knit or purl the remaining 3 stitches together.

Chevron pieces can be combined to create an entire sweater or vest or used as pockets, bands, pillows, shawls, and throws. Stitch patterns that can be incorporated, include simple stripes, garter ridge stitch, slip-stitch patterns, or Fair Isle bands.

CONCLUSION

Bias strips are interesting, fun-to-knit shapes. Experiment by making paper cutouts, or drawing them on grid paper (page 114) or a computer paint program and arranging them into various designs.

PATTERNS

Aidan's Hat (page 102), is made of 2 strips that are joined together with the 3-needle bind-off, the Sonata Shawl (page 103), of 2. In Sonoma (page 104), you combine 4 bias strips with triangles and straight strips for a graceful vest.

Two parallelograms form a chevron

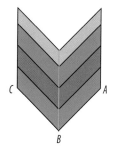

Working a chevron from A to C

Chevron with squared-off edges

Chevron top, squared-off bottom

Add pattern

1 Knit bias strip.

2 Seam cast-on to bind-off.

3 Fold flat and seam across top from beginning . . .

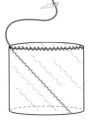

*4 . . . to end.
Do not cut yarn.*

5 Take needle through beginning of seam,

6 Fasten beginning to end, then secure.

7 Finish by blocking.

We couldn't resist trying another version of Ginger's bias-strip hat (Aidan's Hat, on next page). Instead of crisp black and white with red trim, we worked the slip-stitch garter stripes in 2 colorways of Noro's Kureyon. It was such fun. We decided to keep it simple: we joined the strip into a tube, folded it flat, and seamed across. Then we tacked the beginning of the seam to the end. Our hat was complete when we folded up the brim. And look what happened!

Aidan's Hat

Intermediate

One Size

*Measures approximately
22" Around
(Average Adult Size)*

10cm/4"

18 ridges GET GAUGE!

18

over Stripes and Dots Pattern

1 2 3 **4** 5 6

Medium weight

*A 1 Skein
B 1 Skein
C partial Skein*

*4mm/US 6
or size to obtain gauge*

&

*Spare needle
for 3-needle bind-off*

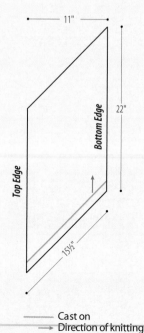

Cast on

→ Direction of knitting

NOTES

1 See *Techniques*, page 116, for Make 1 (M1), ssk, 3-needle bind-off. *2* To increase or decrease the circumference of the hat, knit more or fewer pattern repeats. If you are making the hat considerably smaller, you may want to make it shorter by casting on fewer stitches as well.

STRIPES AND DOTS PATTERN

Note Slip sts as if to purl with yarn to wrong side.
Row 1 (RS) With A, k1, M1, knit to last 3 sts, k2tog, k1.
Row 2 Knit.
Rows 3, 4 With B, repeat Rows 1, 2.
Rows 5, 6 With A, repeat Rows 1, 2.
Row 7 With B, k1, M1, * sl 1, k1; repeat from * until 3 sts remain, k2tog, k1.
Row 8 * K1, sl 1; repeat from *, end k1.
Rows 9, 10 Repeat Rows 1, 2.
Rows 11, 12 Repeat Rows 3, 4.
Repeat Rows 1–12 for pattern.

TO KNIT HAT

With A, cast on 67 sts and knit one row.
Work 12 repeats (144 rows) of Stripes and Dots Pattern, beginning with Row 3.
With A, knit 1 row. Bind off.

TRIMS

Hat edge
With C, pick up 73 sts along top edge.
For smooth edge Bind off.
or for
Picot edge
Knit one row. * Cast on 2 sts, bind off 4 sts. Slip st on right needle to left needle and repeat from *; bind off last st and fasten off.
Bottom band
With A, cast on 13 sts. Knit 12 repeats (144 rows) of Stripes and Dots Pattern, reversing the shaping (ssk at the beginning and M1 at the end of RS rows).
Join band to hat body
With C and WS facing, pick up 73 sts along bottom edge of hat. Set aside. With a separate needle, C, and RS facing, pick up 73 sts along the bottom edge of the band. Working loosely, with RS of hat and

WS of band facing, join the pieces together with a 3-needle bind-off.
Band edge With C, pick up 73 sts along top edge of band. Work Picot edge.

FINISHING

With A, sew cast-on and bound-off edges of hat together. Reverse sewing at band (seam to WS of band). Use pins to mark a line 2" down from top edge of hat. With a tapestry needle and A, sew a line of small running stitches along this line, pull up tightly, tie a knot and sew in the ends. Sew in any remaining ends.

BAABAJOES Wool Pak 8 ply 1 skein each black (A); natural (B); and red (C).

Sometimes one or two modular units are all that is needed to create a unique knit item. Here, two long strips of bias knitting are knit, sewn into rings, then joined, resulting in a striking hat. Instructions for two top edge trim options are given.

Sonata

KNIT ONE, CROCHET TOO: 6 skeins Meringue 904 (A), 8 cones A Taste of Glitz 292 (B)

This dressy evening shawl knits up quickly on two different needle sizes. A version for more casual occasions can easily be made by substituting yarns.

NOTES

1 See *Techniques*, page 116, for cable cast-on. *2* Yarn B is worked holding 3 strands together. *3* Carry unused yarn loosely up edge of knitting. *4* Increases are worked by knitting into the front and back of a stitch (kf&b).

GARTER PATTERN

Rows 1, 2 With A and smaller needles, knit.
Rows 3, 4 With 3 strands of B held together and larger needles, knit.
Repeat Rows 1–4 for pattern.

SECTION 1

Row 1 (RS) With A and smaller needles, cast on 3 sts.
Row 2 Knit.
Row 3 With B and larger needles, kf&b, k1, kf&b— 5 sts.
Row 4 Knit.
Continue in Garter Pattern, AT SAME TIME, k1, kf&b, knit to last 2 sts, kf&b, k1 at beginning and end of every RS row to 55 sts. Work even in pattern, working RS rows as follows:
K1, kf&b, knit to 3 sts before end of row, k2tog, k1.
When piece measures 54" on longest edge, end with 2 rows of A.
Picot Bind-off
With A and smaller needle, k2, bind off 1 st, slip remaining st from right needle to left needle, * cable cast on 2 sts, bind off 4 sts, slip remaining st to left needle; repeat from *, end last repeat by binding off 5 sts.

SECTION 2

Work as Section 1 until piece measures 46". Bind off using Picot Bind-off.

FINISHING

Sew cast-on of Section 2 to long side of Section 1 as shown, loosely stitch through only one strand on the edge of each section.
Sew in ends and block lightly.

Easy

One Size
Measures approximately
Section 1 *54" × 11"*
Section 2 *46" × 11"*

10cm/4"

24 | GET CLOSE
12.5

over Garter Pattern using both needle sizes

1 2 3 **4** 5 6

Medium weight
A *600 yds*

1 2 3 4 5 6

Super Fine weight, used triple
B *1520 yds*

5.5 and 12.75mm/ US 9 and 17
or size to obtain gauge

Cast on
Seam
Direction of knitting

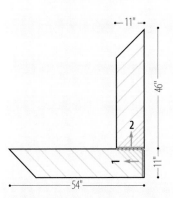

Sonoma

Intermediate

LOOSE FIT

S (M, L)

When buttoned
measures approximately
A 40 (44, 48)"
B 25 (26, 26½)"

10cm/4"

18   GET
GAUGE!
12

over stockinette stitch with A
(knit on RS, purl on WS)

1 2 3 4 **5** 6

Bulky weight

A 190 (210, 230) yds
B 100 (110, 120) yds
C 300 (330, 360) yds

5.5mm/US 9
or size to obtain gauge

5mm/H

Five 20mm/¾" buttons

Stitch holders

NOTES

1 See *Techniques*, page 116, for ssk, Make 1 (M1), p2tog, ssp, S2KP2, and 3-needle bind-off. **2** All increases and decreases are worked one stitch in from the edge.

GARTER RIDGE PATTERN

Rows 1, 3 (RS) Knit.
Row 2 Knit.
Row 4 Purl.
Repeat Rows 1–4 for Garter Ridge Pattern.

LEFT BACK

Row 1 (RS) With C, loosely cast on 32 (34, 36) sts.
Row 2 Knit.
Note In the next section (until shoulder shaping begins), on each RS row, k1, ssk at the beginning of the row and at the end of the row, M1, k1. Work in colors and sts as follows:
* With A, work 14 rows St st; with C, work 2 rows garter st; with B, 2 rows St st; with C, 2 rows garter st; with B, 6 rows St st; with C, 2 rows garter st; repeat from * once. With A, work 14 rows St st.
Shoulder Shaping
Alternating 2 rows garter st in C and 2 rows St st in B, decrease as follows:
K2tog at the end of all RS rows, AT SAME TIME, ssk at the beginning of RS rows in 5 of the next 8 RS rows (dec, dec, no dec, dec, dec, no dec, dec, no dec). Continue in this manner until 13 (15, 17) sts remain. Bind off.

RIGHT BACK

Work as Left Back, reversing shoulder shaping, working M1 at the beginning and k2tog at the end of each RS row.

RIGHT FRONT

Work as Left Back until you reach shoulder shaping. Bind off 12 (14, 16) sts at the beginning of next RS row. Continue with shoulder shaping.

LEFT FRONT

Work as Right Front, reversing shaping. Bind off the 12 (14, 16) neck edge sts on Row 2 of shoulder shaping.

SQUARING OFF THE LOWER EDGE CORNERS

Lower Right Front
Row 1 With C, pick up and knit 48 (50, 52) sts.
Row 2 P1, p2tog, knit to last 3 sts, ssp, p1.
Row 3 Knit to last 3 sts, k2tog, k1.
Row 4 Purl to last 3 sts, ssp, p1.
Continue in Garter Ridge Pattern, AT SAME TIME, decrease as follows:
On the side edge, dec 1 st every 3rd row, keeping the edge st in St st. On the bottom edge, dec 1 st in 3 of 4 rows. Continue until 3 sts remain, work S2KP2, fasten off.
Lower Left Back Edge
Work as Lower Right Front Edge.
Lower Left Front Edge, Lower Right Back Edge
Work as Lower Right Front Edge, reversing shaping.

SIDE SECTIONS

With C, pick up and knit 74 (77, 81) sts along side edge of Right Front.
Knit 1 (3, 5) rows.
Row 1 With C, bind off 18 sts; with A, knit to end.
Row 2 Purl.
Row 3 With C, bind off 6 sts, knit to end.
Row 4 Knit.
Row 5 Bind off 3 sts; with A, knit to end.
Row 6 Purl.
Row 7 With C, bind off 2 sts, knit to end.
Row 8 Knit.
Row 9 With A, bind off 1 st, knit to end.
Row 10 Purl.
Row 11 With C, knit. Put stitches on a holder.
Repeat on Right Back, reversing shaping.
Finish Armhole Edges
With C, pick up and knit 62 sts around armhole opening. Bind off.
Loosely bind off 18 (21, 24) sts at the lower edge of Front and Back side edge (this will form the side slit). With C, join Front and Back side seams together with 3-needle bind-off.
Repeat for Left Front and Back pieces.

JOIN CENTER BACK

With C, pick up sts along Left Back center edge, 13 sts along first A section, 7 sts along B section, 13 sts along A section, 7 sts along B section, 13 sts along

The flattering lines of this diagonally knit vest are emphasized by the use of light and dark tones in the hand-dyed yarns, while side slits add a graceful easy fit.

A section, 9 sts along last B and C section—62 sts. Set needle aside.
With another needle and C, pick up the same number of sts along the Right Back center edge. Join the two sections together with the 3-needle bind-off.

FINISHING
Sew shoulder seams.
Front and Neck Edging
With C, pick up 62 sts along the Right Front center edge, spacing the stitches as they were along the center Back. Pick up 19 (21, 23) sts along right neck, 27 sts across back neck, 19 (21, 23) along left neck, 62 sts along Left Front edge. Bind off.
Button loops
Mark the placement of 5 button loops on Right Front with the first about ½" below the start of the neck shaping. Space the button loops 3¼ (3½, 3¾)" apart. With crochet hook and C, join the yarn to the edge where you want a button loop. Chain 7 and rejoin the yarn in the same space as the first join. Cut the yarn and pull through the loop. Sew on buttons. Block lightly.

——— Cast on
- - - Pick up and knit
→ Direction of knitting

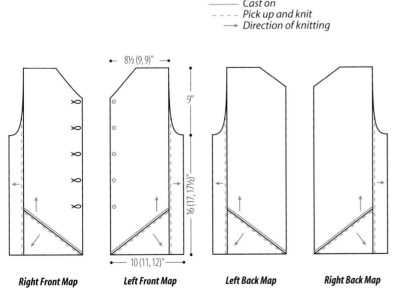

Right Front Map   **Left Front Map**   **Left Back Map**   **Right Back Map**

8½ (9, 9)"
9"
16 (17, 17½)"
10 (11, 12)"

COLINETTE Isis: 3 skeins 90 Venezia (A) and 1 skein 129 Alabaster (B); WigWam 2 skeins 117 Velvet Bilberry (C).

concept to garment

concept to garment

One of the rewards of writing this book has been the emergence of many additional ideas for modular designs. Many of these are currently just sketches that I will revisit and develop later on, but I wanted to discuss some of them in this chapter. They will give you insight into my thought process and show how an idea develops into a module, then into a garment or other project.

When I can't sleep at night, I take up my "theoretical" knitting. I focus on how to create and combine shapes ("What if I knit a T shape, or an H shape…or maybe an L or I-beam shape?"). I seperulate on how to join and arrange them ("Should I pick up stitches on the side, or on the top?"). Sometimes I visualize a project or technique completely, other times I get up and draw it on my computer or on graph paper, or possibly even knit a small sample to test the idea.

For each, I consider factors such as proportion, shaping (how to "build" the shape), and joining possibilities (combining the same or different shapes). This is a stimulating trial-and-error process that frequently yields ideas for more shapes and combinations, some will be discarded and others explored further.

Arrange shapes to create interesting patterns. The units can be lined up side by side, stacked on top of each other, or rotated to the left or right, or upside down. The joining might leave blank areas, the addition of solid-colored shapes to fill the voids can add interest and unity to a design.

BUILDING SHAPES AND MOTIFS

Besides planning the joining of the units for visual appeal, it is also necessary to analyze the knitted shape and consider how the transition from one motif to the next will be made. Consider a T module. The first T is formed by casting on at the base, knitting the stem, increasing on each edge, and knitting the crossbar at the top. The T is rotated counterclockwise and stitches for the next T are cast on and the second T is joined to the first as it is knit.

A large square, composed of four T shapes, can be used in any design involving a square, such as a pillow or a pocket. Several squares can be joined to form a larger piece of fabric, perhaps a throw or afghan.

PLANNING A GARMENT

To make a sweater of these T-squares, the first step is to determine the width and length of the garment. In this example, the design is a short, cropped pullover, 21" long and 21" wide. Draw the outline of the sweater. Next, decide how many times the T-squares will be repeated across the front of the sweater. If the square is repeated three times, each square will be 7" × 7", for a total width of 21".

To determine the exact size of each individual T shape, draw the square on the grid (page 114). The crossbar of the T is three times the width of the base (and the base is the same width as the height of the crossbar). The base of the large square is the width of the

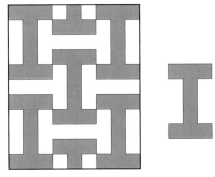
I-Beams, Ts, rectangles and squares

H shapes combined with rectangles and squares

4 L shapes make a square

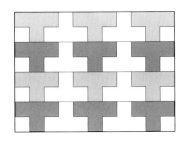
Fabric made of T motifs and squares

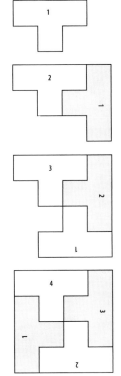

Building a square, one T at a time

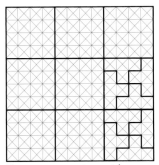

Plan your garment on grid paper
(page 114)

T motifs combine to make a square

crossbar plus the height of the crossbar, or four units wide. 7" ÷ 4 = 1.75", which will be the base number—the width of the base of the T and the height of the crossbar. For this example, the stitch gauge is 5 stitches/inch: 5 × 1.75 = 8.75, which is rounded up to 9. Therefore, cast on 9 stitches for the base of each T shape.

Knit enough rows so that the base is 1.75" high (this depends on the stitch pattern you have chosen), then cast on 9 stitches on each side of the base and knit the same number of rows as in the base of the T. After binding off, rotate the first T, cast on 9 stitches for the next T and begin to knit, joining this new T to the base of the first T at the end of every right-side row. When it's time to cast on stitches for the crossbar of the T, cast on 9 stitches on the right side of the T and pick up 9 sts on the left side of the T. The left edge of this crossbar will also be joined to the first T as the knitting progresses.
Repeat the process to complete four T shapes. Notice that when the fourth T is started, the 9 stitches for the base are picked up, rather than cast on. The base of this last T can be joined to its neighbors on both edges, and the crossbar stitches are picked up on both sides of the base.

To knit the sweater front in this example, make 9 T-squares, joining them using any of the methods discussed in Chapter 1 to form a sweater front. Notice the shoulder shaping, in Chapter 1 I talked about the idea of starting with a simple square or rectangle and then refining it as desired, depending on the design and your knitting ability. In this case, I added neck and shoulder shaping.

REFINING SHAPES AND MOTIFS
In each chapter of this book I focused on a particular modular shape. Some of the patterns incorporate areas of plain knitting to refine the garment shape, such as sleeves or shoulder gussets. A few patterns combine more than one modular shape to create an interesting overall design.

THE PATTERNS
The idea of combining shapes offers a wide array of design possibilities. The Kalapaki Bay Throw, page 94, is an example of such a combination. The motif starts with four mitered squares that are joined to create a larger square. Triangles are the added to the edges of this square, followed by rectangles at the outer edges. The Star Light Star Bright child's sweater, page 92, is another example of combined shapes.

These final ideas and examples are an invitation to you to experiment and play. Who knows where the question "What if….?" might lead?

Allegro

Intermediate

LOOSE FIT

S (M, L)

Measures approximately
A 40 (44, 48)"
B 22 (24, 26)"

10cm/4"

28 | GET GAUGE!

19

over stockinette stitch
(knit on RS, purl on WS)

 1 2 **3** 4 5 6

Light weight
A 750 (900, 1065) yds
B 470 (560, 660) yds

4mm/US 6
or size to obtain gauge

3.75mm/F

&

2 pony beads for front ties

NOTES

1 See *Techniques*, page 116, for Make 1 (M1), ssk, ssp, p2tog, S2PP2, S2KP2, wrap and turn (W&T), 3-needle bind-off, single crochet (sc), backwards crochet, and twisted cord. *2* In these instructions, "pick up" means "pick up and knit." All stitches are picked up with RS facing.

LEFT FRONT

Sections 1 and 2 are worked in St st, alternating 2 rows A with 2 rows B as follows:

Miter 1

Row 1 With B, cast on 95 (107, 115) sts.

Row 2 Knit.

Row 3 With A, k1, ssk, knit to 1 st before center st, S2KP2, knit until 3 sts remain, k2tog, k1.

Row 4 P1, p2tog, purl to 1 st before center st, S2PP2, purl until 3 sts remain, ssp, p1.

Row 5 With B, repeat Row 3.

Row 6 Purl.

Repeat Rows 3–6 until 3 sts remain. S2KP2, fasten off.

Miter 2

With B, pick up 65 (74, 81) sts along Section 1, cast on 46 (51, 55) sts. Work as Section 1, counting first cast-on stitch as the center stitch. Continue in pattern until 16 (19, 21) sts remain on left side of center decrease point. Continue in pattern, EXCEPT instead of decreasing at end on RS rows and beginning of WS rows, M1. This is the bottom of the armhole opening.

Continue in pattern until there are 15 (18, 20) sts before the center st. On this row, omit the increase at left edge; this will give you 15 (18, 20) sts + 1 center st + 15 (18, 20) sts. At this point, resume the original rate of decrease, decreasing at the beginning and end and working a double decrease in the center of the next 3 rows—7 sts remain.

Next WS row P2tog, S2KP2, k2, pass 2 slipped sts over, ssp.

Next row S2KP2, cut yarn and fasten off.

Section 3

Section 3 is worked in garter st, alternating 2 rows A with 2 rows B as follows:

With B, pick up 46 (51, 54) sts along edge of Section 2.

Knit 1 row.

Work M1 increase at beginning of each RS row and decrease 1 st at end of each RS row until 10 (13, 16) garter ridges have been worked.

Continue in garter st, decreasing at the beginning and end of RS rows until 2 sts remain. End k2tog, cut yarn and fasten off.

RIGHT BACK

Work as Left Front.

RIGHT FRONT

Work as Left Front, reversing shaping.

LEFT BACK

Work as Right Front.

BLOCK PIECES

Join the center back seam with 3-needle bind-off.

SHOULDER SHAPING

With B, pick up 14 (16, 18) sts along top of Right Front (see Map).

Knit 1 row.

Short Rows 1, 2 K3 (5, 7), wrap and turn (W&T), knit to end.

Short Rows 3, 4 K7 (9, 11), W&T, knit to end.

Short Rows 5, 6 K11 (13, 15), W&T, knit to end.

Short Rows 7, 8 K14 (16, 18), W&T, knit to end.

Short Rows 9, 10 K11 (13, 15), W&T, knit to end.

Short Rows 11, 12 K7 (9, 11), W&T, knit to end.

Short Rows 13, 14 K3 (5, 7), W&T, knit to end.

Rows 15, 16 Knit all sts.

Bind off.

Repeat this process for the other shoulder, picking up sts on Left Back.

Sew right shoulder to Back and left shoulder to Front.

FINISHING

Sew side seams. With crochet hook and B, work 1 row single crochet and 1 row backwards crochet around armhole edges and outside edge of vest. Sew in ends and block lightly, folding collar back.

Front ties

Cut two strands of A, each 42" long. Make twisted cord of each, sew to center fronts at Miter 2. If desired, thread beads onto end of each tie.

In this unique vest, triangle motifs and mitered corners combine to create flattering diagonal lines. The second version, knit at a larger gauge with heavier yarns and larger needles, is another option in resizing garments. The numbers for size Small were used, but the resulting vest is a Medium.

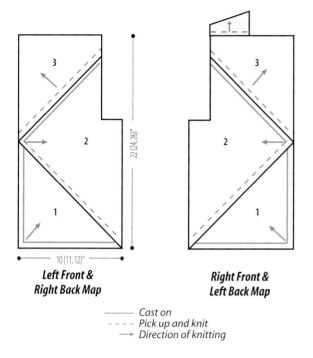

Left Front & Right Back Map

Right Front & Left Back Map

———— Cast on
– – – – Pick up and knit
⟶ Direction of knitting

22 (24, 26)"

10 (11, 12)"

MOUNTAIN COLORS Mountain Goat 4 (4, 5) skeins Flathead Cherry (A); 2 (3, 3) skeins Mountain Twilight (B); shown in size Small

GREAT ADIRONDACK YARN COMPANY Chamois 8 (9, 11) skeins Spring Garden (A) and Newport 3 (3, 4) skeins Eggplant; at a gauge of 17 stitches to 10 cm/4"

T-Square

Intermediate

One Size
Measures approximately
14" × 14"

10cm/4"

36 *GET CLOSE*
19
over Pattern 1

1 2 3 **4** 5 6

Medium weight
A *110 yds*
B *110 yds*
C *110 yds*

4.5mm/US 7 circular,
or size to obtain gauge
40cm (16") long

4mm/G-6

&

14" pillow form
Fabric for pillow back
Extra needle for pick up

NOTES
1 See *Techniques*, page 116, for cable cast-on, S2P2, S2KP2, single crochet, and backwards single crochet. **2** Use cable cast-on throughout. **3** Slip sts purlwise with yarn to WS. **4** In these instructions "pick up" means "pick up and knit." Pick up all stitches with RS facing. **5** Yarn allowance is for Pillow Front, additional yarn will be required to knit the Pillow Back.

PATTERN 1
Row 1 Knit.
Row 2 P1, knit to last st, p1.
Row 3 (RS) * K1, sl 1; repeat from *, end k1.
Row 4 * P1, sl 1; repeat from *, end p1.
Repeat Rows 1–4 for pattern.

PATTERN 2
Row 1 (RS) With C, * p2, k2; repeat from * to last 2 sts, end p2. Do not turn work; slide to other end of circular needle.
Row 2 (RS) With B, p2, * sl 2 with yarn in back (wyib), p2; repeat from *. Turn work.
Row 3 (WS) With C, * k2, p2; repeat from *, end k2. Do not turn work; slide to other end of needle.
Row 4 (WS) With B, * k2, sl 2 with yarn in front (wyif); repeat from *, end k2. Turn work.
Repeat Rows 1–4 for pattern.

PILLOW FRONT
Beginning with module T-1 and following the numbers on Map 1, work as follows:
T-1
13-st section
Row 1 With A, cast on 13 sts.
Beginning with Row 2, work 19 more rows in Pattern 1, end with Row 4.
35-st section
Begin next row Cast on 11 sts, knit across these sts, k13, cast on 11 sts—35 sts. Beginning with Row 2, work 21 rows in Pattern 1, end with Row 2. Bind off.

T-2
Row 1 With B, pick up 13 sts along T-1. Work as T-1, EXCEPT work Rows 1 and 2 with B and Rows 3 and 4 with C and join the left edge of this 13-st

section to T-1 as follows: slip last st wyif, pick up a st purlwise on edge of T-1 and p2tog with the slipped st. Pick up last 11 sts for 35-st section along edge of T-1.

T-3
Using only A, work as T-2, picking up and joining sts as shown on Map 1.

T-4
With B and C, work as T-2, breaking yarn after 13-st section, then beginning 35-st section by picking up first 11 sts along T-1, k13, then pick up last 11 sts along T-3. When T-4 is completed, sew its right edges to T-1 (see Map 1).

PILLOW EDGING
Row 1 With B, pick up 46 sts along any edge of the pillow top (see Map 2).
Row 2 Knit.
Work 12 rows of Pattern 2, 8 rows with C and B, then 4 rows with A and B. With A, knit 2 rows. Bind off.
Repeat for other edges.

CORNERS
Row 1 With B, pick up 17 sts along two sides of any pillow corner (see Map 3).
Row 2 Knit.
Row 3 With C, knit until 1 st before center st, S2KP2, knit remaining sts.
Row 4 Knit to center st, p1, knit remaining sts.
Rows 5, 6 With B, repeat Rows 3, 4.
Rows 7–10 Repeat Rows 3–6.
Rows 11–14 With A, repeat Rows 3–6.
Rows 15, 16 Repeat Rows 3, 4.
Row 17 Slip 2 as if to purl, p2, pass slipped sts over. Fasten off.

FINISHING
With B, work 1 row single crochet and 1 row backwards crochet around entire piece.

Four interlocking T shapes are rotated to form a square in this quick-to-knit pillow. For a strong geometric finish, striped rectangles frame its sides and mitered squares fill its corners.

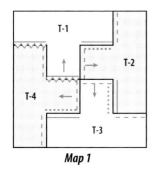

Map 1

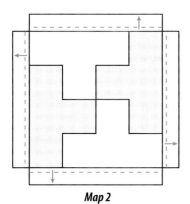

Map 2

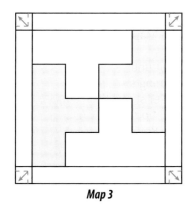

Map 3

Bryspun Kid-n-Ewe 1 ball each rust 510 (A), black 110 (B), and turquoise 490 (C).

Color Key

☐ A

▨ 2 rows B, 2 rows C

───── Cast on
- - - - Pick up and knit
.... P2tog join
∿∿∿ Seam
⟶ Direction of knitting

Suggestions for Pillow Back
Pillow Front can be sewn to a fabric-covered pillow form, to a fabric back, or to a knitted back. For the Back, you could duplicate the Front, work a square in Pattern 1, or try another block design.

Tumbling Triangles, p. 28

Sonoma, p. 104

Nicole's Cardigan, p. 18

Yuba River, p. 54

Morgan's Pullover, p. 78

Mendocino, p. 64

Arnie's Vest, p. 16

T-Square, p. 112

Nevada City Windows, p. 20

Star Light, p. 92

Please feel free to photocopy these 2 pages for your use in planning modular knits

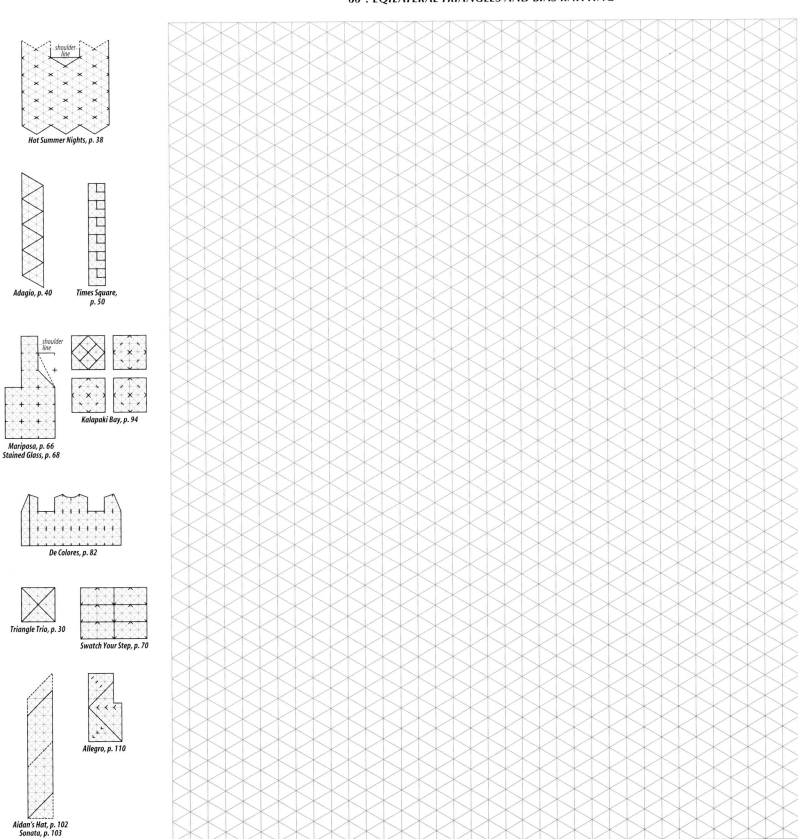

Hot Summer Nights, p. 38

Adagio, p. 40

Times Square, p. 50

shoulder line

Mariposa, p. 66
Stained Glass, p. 68

Kalapaki Bay, p. 94

De Colores, p. 82

Triangle Trio, p. 30

Swatch Your Step, p. 70

Allegro, p. 110

Aidan's Hat, p. 102
Sonata, p. 103

*Bias knitting can range from 0°—90° ; 60° is a good starting point

Techniques

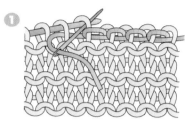

CABLE CAST-ON

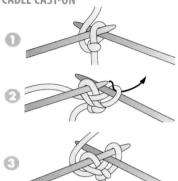

CAST-ONS

Cable cast-on *Uses* A cast-on that is useful when adding stitches within the work.

1 Make a slipknot on left needle.

2 Working into this knot's loop, knit a stitch and place it on left needle.

3 Insert right needle between the last 2 stitches. From this position, knit a stitch and place it on left needle. Repeat Step 3 for each additional stitch.

Or, if adding to existing stitches, hold needle with stitches in left-hand and work Step 3 for each additional stitch.

Pick up

In this book, "pick up" means "pick up and knit," and stitches are usually picked up 1 stitch in from edge, as shown in illustration 2.

1 Illustration shows stitches being picked up *into* first stitch of stockinette stitch, 3 stitches for every 4 rows.

2 For a firmer edge, pick up 1 stitch in from edge.

PICK UP

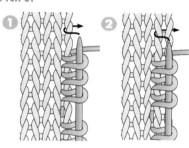

BIND-OFFS

3-needle bind-off *Uses* A substitute for seaming.

1, 2 *Ridge on RS* With stitches from one piece of knitting on one needle and stitches from another on a second needle, place *wrong sides together and right side facing you*. * K2tog (1 from front needle and 1 from back needle); repeat from * once. Pass first stitch on right needle over 2nd stitch. Continue to k2tog (1 front stitch and 1 back stitch) and bind off across.

3 *Ridge on WS* Work as above but with right sides together and wrong side facing.

Sewn bind-off

1 With a separate piece of yarn and darning needle, *slip needle into first stitch as if to knit and slip stitch off needle.

2 Slip needle into next 2 stitches as if to purl and pull through, leaving stitches on needle. Repeat from *. End slip needle into last stitch as if to purl. Fasten off.

Standard bind-off

1, 2 Knit the first 2 stitches; insert left needle into first stitch on right needle and pull it over the second stitch and completely off the needle: one stitch bound off.

3 Knit one more stitch, insert left needle into first stitch on right needle, and pull it over the new stitch and off the needle.

4 Repeat Step 3. When last loop is on right needle, break yarn and pull tail of yarn through loop to fasten.

3-NEEDLE BIND-OFF

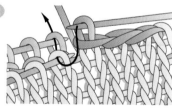

ridge on RS

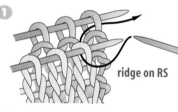

ridge on WS

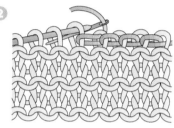

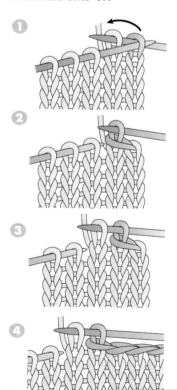

P2TOG

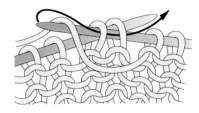

S2PP2

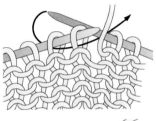

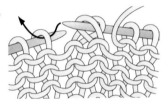

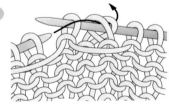

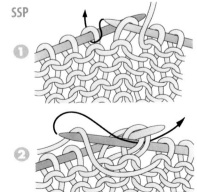

SSP

DECREASES

P2tog *Uses* A left-slanting single decrease.
Purl 2 stitches together; 2 stitches become one.

S2KP2, SSKP, sl2-k1-p2sso *Uses* A centered double decrease.
1 Slip 2 stitches together to right needle as if to knit.
2 Knit next stitch.
3 Pass 2 slipped stitches over knit stitch and off right needle.
4 Completed: 3 stitches become 1; the center stitch is on top.

S2PP2 *Uses* A centered double decrease worked on the purl side.
1 Slip 2 stitches seperately to right needle as if to knit.
2 Slip these 2 stitches back onto left needle. Insert right needle through their 'back' loops, into the second stitch and then the first and slip 2 sts to right needle.
3 Purl next st.
4 Pass 2 slipped sts over purl st and off right needle. 3 sts become 1; the center st is on top.

ssk *Uses* A left-slanting single decrease.
1 Slip 2 stitches separately to right needle as if to knit.
2 Knit these 2 stitches together by slipping left needle into them from left to right; 2 stitches become one.

ssp *Uses* A left-slanting single decrease.
1 Slip 2 stitches separately to right needle as if to knit.
2 Slip these 2 stitches back onto left needle. Insert right needle through their 'back' loops, into the second stitch and then the first. Purl them together.

sssk *Uses* A left-slanting double decrease.
Work same as ssk except:
1 Slip 3 stitches separately to right needle as if to knit.
2 Knit these 3 stitches together by slipping left needle into them from left to right; 3 stitches become one.

S2KP2, SSKP, SL2-K1-P2SSO

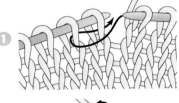

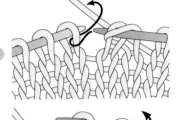

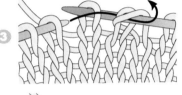

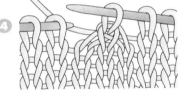

SSK

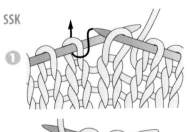

LIFTED INCREASE

right knit increase
RKI

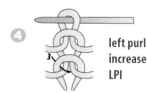
left knit increase
LKI

right purl increase
RPI

left purl increase
LPI

YARN OVER BEFORE A KNIT

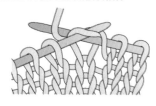

YARN OVER BEFORE A PURL

INCREASES

Lifted increase

If instructions don't specify, use right knit increase.

Knit

For a right increase: knit into right loop of stitch in row below next stitch on left needle (1), then knit stitch on needle (2).

For a left increase: knit one stitch, then knit into left loop of stitch in row below last stitch knitted (3).

Purl

For a right increase: purl into right loop of stitch in row below next stitch on left needle (1), then purl stitch on needle (2).

For a left increase: purl one stitch, then purl into left loop of stitch in row below last stitch purled (3).

Make 1 (M1, M1K) *Uses* A single increase.

1 *For a left-slanting increase (M1L):* with left needle from front of work, pick up strand between last stitch knitted and next stitch. Knit, twisting the strand by working into the loop at the back of the needle.

2 This is the completed increase.

3 *For a right-slanting increase (M1R):* with left needle from back of work, pick up strand between last stitch knitted and next stitch. Knit, twisting the strand by working into the loop at the front of the needle.

4 This is the completed increase.

Make 1 purl (M1P)

Occasionally instructions specify to work a Make 1 increase in purl.

For a left-slanting increase: Work as for Make 1, Step 1, except purl, twisting the strand by working into the loop at the back of the needle.

For a right-slanting increase: Work as for Make 1, Step 3, except purl.

Yarn over

Before a knit; With yarn in front of needle, knit next stitch.

Before a purl; With yarn in front of needle, bring yarn over needle and to front again, purl next stitch.

MISCELLANEOUS

Grafting *Uses* An invisible method of joining knitting horizontally, row to row. Useful at shoulders, underarms, and tips of mittens, socks, and hats.

Stockinette graft:

1 Arrange stitches on two needles.

2 Thread a blunt needle with matching yarn (approximately 1" per stitch).

3 Working from right to left, with right sides facing you, begin with Steps 3a and 3b:

3a Front needle: yarn through 1st stitch as if to purl, leave stitch on needle.

3b Back needle: yarn through 1st stitch as if to knit, leave on.

4 Work 4a and 4b across:

4a Front needle: through 1st stitch as if to knit, slip off needle; through next st as if to purl, leave on needle.

4b Back needle: through 1st stitch as if to purl, slip off needle; through next st as if to knit, leave on needle.

5 Adjust tension to match rest of knitting.

Knit through back loop (tbl)

To knit into the back of a stitch, insert the needle into the stitch from right to left.

Make 1

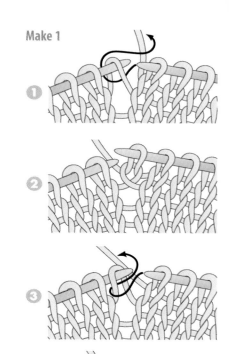

① ② ③ ④

GRAFTING

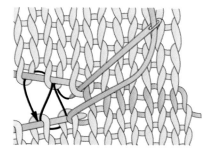

KNIT THROUGH BACK LOOP

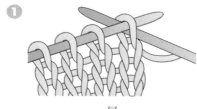
① ②

TWISTED CORD

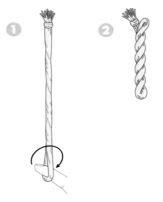

Twisted cord

1 Cut strands 6 times the length of cord needed. Fold in half and knot the cut ends together.

2 With knotted end in left hand and right index finger in folded end, twist clockwise until cord is tightly twisted.

3 Fold cord in half and smooth as it twists on itself; knot.

MATTRESS STITCH

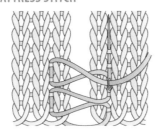

Mattress stitch

Mattress stitch seams are good all-purpose seams. They require edge stitches (which are taken into the seam allowance) and are worked with the right sides facing.

1 After blocking, thread blunt needle with matching yarn.

2 Working between edge stitch and next stitch, pick up 2 bars.

3 Cross to matching place in opposite piece, and pick up 2 bars.

4 Return to first piece, go down into the hole you came out of, and pick up 2 bars.

5 Return to opposite piece, go down into the hole you came out of, and pick up 2 bars.

6 Repeat Steps 4 and 5 across, pulling thread very tight, then stretching the seam slightly.

WRAP AND TURN (W&T)

on knit row

Wrap

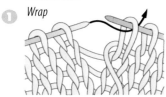

Hide wrap on next knit row

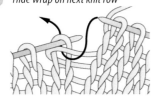

on purl row

Wrap

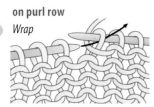

Hide wrap on next purl row

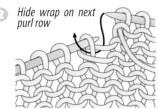

Wrap and turn (W&T) for short rows *Uses* Each short row adds two rows of knitting across a section of the work. Since the work is turned before completing a row, stitches must be wrapped at the turn to prevent holes. Work a wrap in stockinette as follows:

On knit row

1 With yarn in back, slip next stitch as if to purl. Bring yarn to front of work and slip stitch back to left needle as shown. Turn work.

2 When you come to the wrap on the following knit row, make it less visible by knitting the wrap together with the stitch it wraps.

On purl row

1 With yarn in front, slip next stitch as if to purl. Bring yarn to back of work and slip stitch back to left needle as shown. Turn work.

2 When you come to the wrap on the following purl row, make it less visible by inserting right needle under wrap as shown, placing the wrap on the left needle, and purling it together with the stitch it wraps.

CROCHET

Single crochet (SC)

Work slip stitch to begin. 1 Insert hook into next stitch.

2 Yarn over and through stitch; 2 loops on hook.

3 Yarn over and through both loops on hook; single crochet completed.

Repeat Steps 1–3.

Backwards single crochet

1 Work from left to right.

1a Work a slip stitch to begin.

1b Insert hook into next stitch to right.

2 Bring yarn through stitch only. As soon as hook clears the stitch, flip your wrist (and the hook). There are now two loops on the hook, and the just-made loop is to the front of the hook (left of the old loop).

3 Yarn over and through both loops on hook; one backwards single crochet completed.

4 Continue working to right, repeating from Step 1b.

SINGLE CROCHET

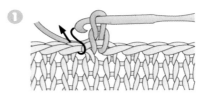

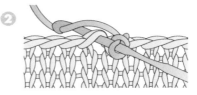

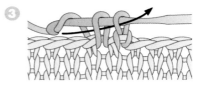

BACKWARDS SINGLE CROCHET

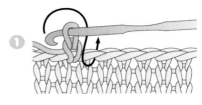

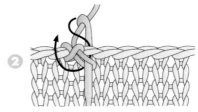

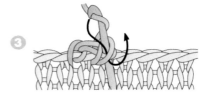

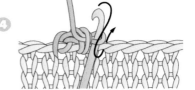

Specifications: At a Glance

Use the charts and guides below to make educated decisions
about yarn thickness, needle size, garment ease, and pattern options.

Understanding pattern specifications

Intermediate ◄ **Skill level**

LOOSE FIT

M (L, 1X)

Measures approximately
A 45½ (49, 52½)"
B 24¼ (26, 27¾)"

◄ **Fit**
Includes ease (additional width) built into pattern.

◄ **Sizing**

Garment measurements
at the A, B, & C lines on the fit icon

10cm/4"

20 ridges GET GAUGE!
19

*over garter stitch
(knit all rows)*

◄ **Gauge**
The number of stitches and rows you need in 10 cm or 4", worked as specified.

1 2 3 **4** 5 6 ◄ **Yarn weight**
and amount in yards

Medium weight
350 (400, 450) yds

◄ **Type of needles**
Straight, unless circular or double-pointed are recommended.

*4mm/US 6
or size to obtain gauge*

&

◄ **Any extras**

Stitch markers

Fit

STANDARD FIT

LOOSE FIT

OVERSIZED FIT

CLOSE FIT

Measuring

- **A** Bust/Chest
- **B** Body length
- **C** Center back to cuff (arm slightly bent)

Needles

US 0 2	MM
1	2.25
2	2.75
3	3.25
4	3.5
5	3.75
6	4
7	4.5
8	5
9	5.5
10	6
10½	6.5
11	8
13	9
15	10
17	12.75

Equivalent weights

¾ oz		20 g
1 oz		28 g
1½ oz		40 g
1¾ oz		50 g
2 oz		60 g
3½ oz		100 g

Sizing
Measure around the fullest part of your bust/chest to find your size.

Children	4	6	8	10
Actual chest	23"	25"	26.5"	28"

Women	XXS	XS	Small	Medium	Large	1X	2X	3X
Actual bust	28"	30"	32–34"	36–38"	40–42"	44–46"	48–50"	52–54"

Men	Small	Medium	Large	1X	2X
Actual chest	34–36"	38–40"	42–44"	46–48"	50–52"

Conversion chart

centimeters	0.394	inches
grams	0.035	ounces
inches	X 2.54 =	centimeters
ounces	28.6	grams
meters	1.1	yards
yards	.91	meters

Modules: At a Glance

For more information on modular shapes, turn to the page references listed.

Yarn weight categories

Yarn Weight

Super Fine	Fine	Light	Medium	Bulky	Super Bulky

Also called

Sock Fingering Baby	Sport Baby	DK Light-Worsted	Worsted Afghan Aran	Chunky Craft Rug	Bulky Roving

Stockinette Stitch Gauge Range 10cm/4 inches

27 sts to 32 sts	23 sts to 26 sts	21 sts to 24 sts	16 sts to 20 sts	12 sts to 15 sts	6 sts to 11 sts

Recommended needle (metric)

2.25 mm to 3.25 mm	3.25 mm to 3.75 mm	3.75 mm to 4.5 mm	4.5 mm to 5.5 mm	5.5 mm to 8 mm	8 mm and larger

Recommended needle (US)

1 to 3	3 to 5	5 to 7	7 to 9	9 to 11	11 and larger

Locate the Yarn Weight and Stockinette Stitch Gauge Range over 10cm to 4" on the chart. Compare that range with the information on the yarn label to find an appropriate yarn. These are guidelines only for commonly used gauges and needle sizes in specific yarn categories.

Shapes

Squares, page 10

 Square 1 Cast on. * Knit until the piece is as long as it is wide. Bind off.

 Square 2 Turn 90 degrees. Pick up the number of stitches that were cast on for Square 1. Repeat from * .

Rectangles, page 10, and Straight Strips, page 74
Cast on and knit to desired length.

Right Triangles (90 and 45 degree), page 24

 In garter stitch, decrease (ssk) at the beginning. **or,** k2tog at the end of every other row.

In stockinette stitch, decrease (ssk or k2tog) on 3 of every 4 rows; on purl rows, work ssp for left-slanting decrease or p2tog for right-slanting decrease.

Equilateral Triangles (60 degree), page 34

 In garter stitch, ssk at the beginning and k2tog at the end of every 4th row.

In stockinette stitch, decrease every other row.

Mitered Squares, page 44

In garter stitch, decrease 2 stitches in center of row, every other row.

In stockinette stitch, decrease in 3 of every 4 rows.

Hypotenuse

Wondering how many stitches to pick up on a diagonal? Here's a handy table (no need for math)

□ *x 1.4 =* ⊠

⊠ *÷ 1.4 =* □

□	⊠
1	1
2	3
3	4
4	6
5	7
6	8
7	10
8	11
9	13
10	14
11	15
12	17
13	18
14	20
15	21
16	22
17	24
18	25
19	27
20	28

For larger numbers, just do the addition:

If straight edge is 29 sts:

20	28
+ 9	+13
29	41

Pick up 41 sts on diagonal.

Aurora Yarns PO Box 3068, Moss Beach, CA 94038
Baabajoes Wool Co. 1720 Robb St. #11-103, Lakewood, CO 8021
Berroco 14 Elmdale Rd., Uxbridge, MA 01569
Brown Sheep Co 100662 County Road 16, Mitchell, NE 69357
Bryson Distributing 7376 Almaden St. #39-40, Eugene, OR 97402
Cascade Yarns PO Box 58168, Tuckwila, WA 98138
Cherry Tree Hill PO Box 659, Barton, VT 05822
Cochenille Design Studio PO Box 234276, Encinitas, CA 92023
Fiesta Yarns 5401 San Diego NE, Ste. A, Albuquerque, NM 87113

Great Adirondack 950 Co Hwy 126, Amsterdam, NY 02010
Knit One Crochet Too 7 Commons Ave, Ste. 2, Windham, ME 04062
Knitting Fever 35 Debevoise Ave, Roosevelt, NY 11575
Lorna's Laces 4229 N. Honore St., Chicago, IL 60613
Lucci Yarn Inc. 202-91 Rocky Hill Rd., Bayside, NY 11361
Mountain Colors PO Box 156, Corvallis, MT 59828
Russi Sales 605 Clark Rd., Bellingham, WA 98225
Unique Kolours 28 North Bacton Hill Rd., Malvern, PA 19355

To my teachers, especially those who have encouraged me to explore and ask "What if...?"

As with most books, the labor, support, inspiration, and ideas of many people have gone into the creation of Module Magic. This book is dedicated to my teachers, those who have taught and influenced me in academic settings and in various workshops and seminars throughout my life. These include Esther Dendel, the beloved leader of the Thursday morning workshops in southern California, Dr. David Cole at Occidental College, Clinton McKenzie at California State University, Fullerton, Elizabeth Zimmerman, who influenced my knitting education through her many books and articles. The support and advice of friends and colleagues, including Susan Lazear, Ruth Lantz, and Sally Melville, has been invaluable, as well as that of my friends in my creativity group.

Thanks also go to the knitters (and friends) who helped with many of the garments and patterns in the book. They are Dee Jones, Eileen Lee, and Barbara Langdon. What can I say about the talented staff at XRX, without whom there would be no book. Thanks especially to Elaine Rowley for her impressive editing skills, Alexis Xenakis for his amazing photographs, David Xenakis for color corrections (and for sharing his extensive Photoshop knowledge!), Natalie Sorenson for her charming sketches, Sue Nelson, Rick Mondragon, and Bob Natz.

Finally, thanks and love go to my ever-supportive husband, Arnie, who has heard, "Just let me finish this row", so very many times.

Author Ginger Luters and photographer Alexis Xenakis